ESSENTIALS

of Managing

Corporate Cash

Michèle Allman-Ward
James Sagner

WILEY

John Wiley & Sons, Inc.

Copyright © 2003 by John Wiley & Sons, Inc., Hoboken, New Jersey. All rights reserved.

Published simultaneously in Canada

For general information on our other products and services, or technical support, please contact our Customer Care Department within the United States at 800-762-2974, outside the United States at 317-572-3993 or fax 317-572-4002.

Wiley also publishes its books in a variety of electronic formats. Some content that appears in print may not be available in electronic books.

For more information about Wiley products, visit our Web site *www.wiley.com*.

Library of Congress Cataloging-in-Publication Data:

Allman-Ward, Michèle.
   Essentials of managing corporate cash / Michèle Allman-Ward, James Sagner.
     p. cm.
   ISBN 0-471-20875-2 (PAPER : alk. paper)
  1. Cash management—United States.   I. Sagner, James   II. Title.
   HG4028.C45 A455 2003
   658.15′5—dc21   2002014908

Printed in the United States of America

10 9 8 7 6 5 4 3 2 1

Contents

Preface

This book is one of a series on essentials of business management. The importance of managing corporate cash has given rise to the treasury and cash management professions. Why does this industry warrant an entire book? Aren't businesspeople already knowledgeable about how to organize their treasury function and handle their funds?

In preparing this material—the first new treatment since James Sagner's *Cashflow Reengineering* (AMACOM, 1997)—the authors began by listing the major developments in just the past five years:

- The deregulation of financial services due to the Riegle-Neal Act of 1994 and the Gramm-Leach-Bliley Act of 1999

- The complete change in the corporate-banking relationship from a buyer's to a seller's market

- Globalization of world business, including the creation of the economic monetary union in Europe and its single currency, the euro

- The emphasis on new treasury structures to better manage resources on a worldwide basis

- The developing interest in e-commerce for business-to-business (B2B) transactions, which changes how data and funds flow and greatly reduces working capital cycle time

- The emergence of the "new economy" with its orientation to information and cash, driving finance into every area of a company

Treasury operations today bear little resemblance to the function of just a few years ago. Instead of issuing checks and worrying about the depositing of incoming cash, the treasury manager of the twenty-first century has become integrated to every facet of the business. In this environment, line and staff separations and the "silo" effect of autonomous strategic business units (SBUs) have become meaningless. Effective cash management has become fundamental to a company's underlying health and survival.

This book is a back-to-basics guide and reference to the new cash management profession for managers who find themselves with treasury responsibilities. Insights are provided to the cash management world, the important terminology, and strategies that work.

In planning the content, the authors had in mind the needs of a number of different groups:

- New members of the profession, including students and cash management apprentices
- Current financial managers who need a succinct, well-written reference
- Members of allied professions (e.g., accountants, information specialists, attorneys) who wish to expand their knowledge base
- Professionals who find themselves managing the treasury function, but who do not have a treasury background and need an easy-to-absorb, nontechnical guide to the essentials
- Readers outside of the United States who expect to do business in this country
- Senior managers who need an "executive summary" in order to understand cash management without becoming enmeshed in the details

Essentials of Managing Corporate Cash is organized in the following sequence:

- Chapter 1 introduces the concept of twenty-first century treasury management as a discipline and as a profession.

- Chapter 2 examines the paper and electronic payment systems in the United States, and addresses payment system risk.

- Chapter 3 provides an overview of managing cash inflows and important concepts in collection system design.

- Chapter 4 reviews managing cash outflows and the allied topics of concentration and disbursements.

- Chapter 5 takes a closer look at liquidity management and the role of forecasting, borrowing, and investing.

- Chapter 6 examines treasury information systems together with a review of security issues.

- Chapter 7 explores the complex subject of international cash management, risk management, cross-border clearing, payment methods, and some of the latest developments in global cash management.

- Chapter 8 describes the U.S. banking environment, regulations that impact the cash manager, and the account analysis.

- Chapter 9 discusses bank relationship management, the different roles that banks play, the bank selection process, and bank performance evaluation.

- Chapter 10 summarizes trends in treasury organization and cash management and the changes that can be expected in the industry.

In the appendices the reader will find additional useful sources of information.

Acknowledgments

The authors acknowledge the hundreds of clients who have given them their trust and confidence over the years. Businesspeople have taught us far more than we have taught them. Specific thanks are as follows:

- Allman-Ward is grateful to her long-suffering former bosses from Bank of Boston, Bankers Trust, J.P. Morgan, and First Interstate, who continue to be supportive.

- Sagner thanks his former colleagues from the First National Bank of Chicago (now Bank One) and current Sagner/Marks partners.

- Both authors are appreciative of the efforts of Timothy Burgard of John Wiley & Sons, Inc., who shepherded this book through to publication.

Certain of the material in Chapter 7 previously appeared as an article by Allman-Ward in the *Global Treasury News* Web site (*www.gtnews.com*). Her appreciation to that source is hereby acknowledged.

Allman-Ward also wishes to acknowledge the following publications as sources of reference: Richard Bort's *Corporate Cash Management Handbook,* Kenneth L. Parkinson & Jarl G. Kallbergs' *Corporate Liquidity, Essentials of Cash Management* published by the Association for Financial Professionals, and *The Federal Reserve System—Purposes and Functions,* published by the Board of Governors of the Federal Reserve System.

To Michèle's husband Peter and her parents Keith and Denise Lawley
. . . and to all of our friends in the treasury management profession

CHAPTER 1

Introduction to Managing Corporate Cash

After reading this chapter, you will be able to

- Understand the importance of managing corporate cash and how cash management is instrumental to the ongoing operations of a company
- Appreciate why cash managers are needed and the role they play in managing the day-to-day cash position and liquidity of the company
- Review the historical evolution of cash management through to the current day
- Learn the major terms, concepts, and objectives of cash management

This chapter introduces the topics that will be developed more fully throughout the book.

CASE STUDY

Bill Fold is the treasurer of a diversified manufacturing and distributing company, General Trading and Delivery (GETDOE), that operates on a decentralized basis. The company grew primarily through acquisition of complementary businesses, with an assurance of minimal interference from corporate headquarters. To date, the company's cash management has been handled very autonomously. Although other functions such as technology, legal, and internal auditing have been centralized to achieve efficiencies and economies of scale, treasury remains highly decentralized.

Bill finds himself with an almost continuous liquidity problem, and is under daily pressure from the business units for operating funds and investment capital for plant and equipment. Meanwhile, the bankers are pressuring Bill for more noncredit business to augment the slim margins on the credit lines; and his boss, the chief financial officer, is demanding better and timelier information on the company's finances.

Bill believes the time has come for the treasury to be managed more efficiently in order to release the pockets of "unused" cash he suspects are hidden within the company. In order to analyze the current activities and to begin initiating improvements, Bill hires a cash manager with considerable experience, Ann I. Shade. Ann has been a cash manager for over 10 years and looks forward to the challenge of applying her skills in the new company.

What Is Cash Management?

Cash management is the art—and increasingly the science—of managing a company's short-term resources to sustain its ongoing activities, mobilize funds, and optimize liquidity. The most important elements are:

- The efficient utilization of current assets and current liabilities of a firm throughout each phase of the business operating cycle

- The systematic planning, monitoring, and management of the company's collections, disbursements, and account balances

- The gathering and management of information to use available funds effectively and identify risk

Exhibit 1.1 presents the cash management model and illustrates how the primary cash management functions interrelate.

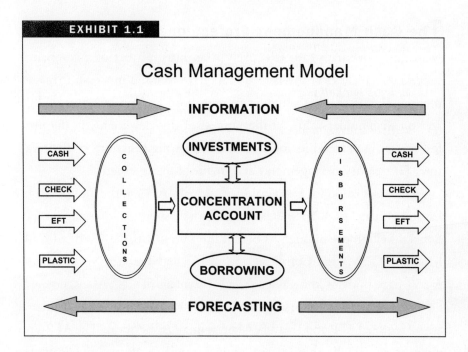

EXHIBIT 1.1

Cash Management Model

Cash management comprises at least nine major functions:

1. Accelerating and efficiently collecting cash inflows

2. Concentrating collected funds

3. Controlling the timing of cash outflows

4. Forecasting the cash position

5. Securing adequate sources of short-term funds

6. Optimizing use of any temporary cash surpluses

7. Gathering timely information

8. Implementing the systems and services necessary to monitor, manage, and control the cash position

9. Ensuring the internal and external transfer of financial data

Each of these functions will be discussed in greater detail when reviewing the responsibilities of the cash manager later in this chapter.

The Cash Management Profession

Managing corporate cash effectively is an integral part of a company's success. Advances over the last 50 years have resulted in a cash management discipline that has a significant impact on a company's bottom line and on shareholder value. In the process of this development, the profession has broadened its focus to encompass the functions of the treasurer (as treasury management) and financial management.

The Association for Financial Professionals (AFP) in the United States has more than 14,000 members and provides a source of ongoing professional development through its certification programs, the Certified Cash Manager (CCM) and Certificate in Finance and Treasury Management. A 550-page body of knowledge called "Essentials of Cash Management," now in its seventh edition, supports the CCM program. In addition, there are 62 regional AFP and Treasury Management Associations. The AFP also supports its membership by providing financial tools and publications, career development, continuing education, research, representation to legislators and regulators, and the development of industry standards.

The Association of Corporate Treasurers (ACT) is an international organization with 18 regional groups in the United Kingdom and overseas. The ACT's objective is to encourage and promote the study and practice of corporate treasury management and related subjects. It offers extensive training opportunities and treasury-related publications. The ACT's Certificate in International Cash Management (Cert CM) is offered in locations around the globe.

Technology, too, has been putting tools in the hands of cash managers, and providing solutions for the analysis and management of a company's cash position. Globalization, on the other hand, has added complexity and new challenges, requiring knowledge of the cross-border management of funds and understanding of the implications of tax and risk exposure in the broader international environment.

Historical Perspective

The birth of cash management can be traced back more than half of a century when, in 1947, RCA became one of the first companies to use a lockbox to accelerate collection of payments from dealers. According to the "Global Payments 2000/1 Report" of the Boston Consulting Group, by the year 2008, the worldwide cash management revenue associated with domestic and cross-border payments is estimated to reach almost $310 billion per year.

Prior to the late 1940s, interest rates were low—in March 1948, the three-month U.S. Treasury Bill rate first rose to 1 percent—and there was little incentive to manage cash flows on an active basis. However, when interest rates began to rise in the late 1960s—the three-month Treasury Bill rate was almost 8 percent by the end of the decade—banks developed new investment vehicles to attract funds, such as the negotiable certificate of deposit, and companies began to manage cash more aggressively.

The 1970s saw the wide-spread use of one of the first major technological innovations in cash management: the lockbox model. These computer programs used mail times between cities and bank availability schedules (see Chapter 3) to develop optimal lockbox locations to minimize total collection float.

The 1980s produced a combination of conditions that encouraged the rapid adoption of cash management techniques:

- Significant inflation, driven to a large extent by the OPEC oil embargo of 1973–1974

- High interest rates, with the prime rate reaching nearly 20 percent by 1980

- Financial innovation, including the first products to cross traditional financial services boundaries, such as Merrill Lynch's cash management account (CMA)

- Technological advances in electronic banking, including treasury information systems (see Chapter 6) and the introduction of automated teller machines (ATMs)

Financial innovation gave rise to new products and services to meet the needs of the corporate customer, including:

- *Remote (later, "controlled") disbursement.* Exploited the time checks take to clear
- *Depository Transfer Checks (later ACHs).* Permitted the transfer of funds from local collection banks to concentration banks
- *Automated Clearing House (ACH) transfers.* Introduced an electronic payment alternative to wire transfers for low-value, nonurgent transfers
- *Bank balance reporting.* Provided previous day balances and transaction detail electronically
- *Commercial paper.* Offered large companies a less expensive short-term borrowing alternative to traditional bank lending

In the 1980s, the personal computer (PC), which later spawned the treasury workstation (TWS), began the revolution that would transform the role of the cash manager from a gatherer of data to an analyzer and user of information. With the TWS performing the routine data-gathering functions, the liberated cash manager now focuses on interpretation of trends, forecasting, risk management, and the optimization of liquidity.

During the 1990s, technological developments progressed even more rapidly, and deregulation of the banking industry continued. The most significant milestones of this decade were:

- The Interstate Banking and Branch Efficiency Act of 1994 effectively replaced the 1927 McFadden Act, permitting banks to branch nationwide by 1997 (see Chapter 8).
- The 1933 Glass-Steagall Act was repealed by the passage of the Gramm-Leach-Bliley Act (1999). This legislation deregulated

financial services and permitted such mergers as that between Travelers Insurance Company and Citibank, creating the new financial powerhouse, Citigroup (see Chapter 8).

- The development of electronic data interchange (EDI), and its successor electronic commerce (EC), began to change the nature of the trade cycle and how business is conducted (see Chapters 2 and 10).

- The Economic and Monetary Union (EMU) was launched at the end of the last century, introducing a centralized European Central Bank and a single currency, the euro, for 11 European countries. This significant development promises new and future efficiencies in cross-border liquidity management as harmonization continues to evolve throughout the EMU and as new countries join the union (see Chapter 7).

- Technology enabled the centralization of treasury and/or outsourcing of selected functions, such as collections and disbursements, resulting in a more efficient and cost-effective organization.

The trends of the twenty-first century are already emerging. Banks are finding themselves in fierce competition with nonbank providers as suppliers of financial services. At the same time, credit is becoming a scarcer commodity for corporate borrowers, and treasurers are learning to reduce their dependence on cheap short-term loans. The Internet has brought the world to the doorstep of even the smallest company. In addition, the Web is reengineering business processes and the way by which companies assess their core competencies. Cash management is headed for interesting times.

Why Cash Managers Are Needed

The cash manager is responsible for managing the imbalances between a company's cash inflows and cash outflows caused by both the operating cycle and the nature of cash flows. An understanding of both concepts is necessary, in particular how they relate to individual companies and their industry.

The Operating Cycle and the Cash Flow Timeline

For the majority of companies, the operating cycle consists of buying raw materials, converting them into goods and services, and selling the finished goods (see Exhibit 1.2).

The operating cycle, in turn, defines the cash flow timeline, that is, the timing of cash inflows and cash outflows. Exhibit 1.3 illustrates the connection between the operating, cash, trade, and accounting cycles.

The usual pattern is for cash outflows to precede inflows. The purchase of raw materials leads to additional, ongoing expenses associated with the conversion process. A sale does not necessarily result in an immediate cash inflow. A company will need sufficient liquidity to finance the operations until funds are actually collected. Each industry will have its own pattern of cash and operating cycles.

EXHIBIT 1.2

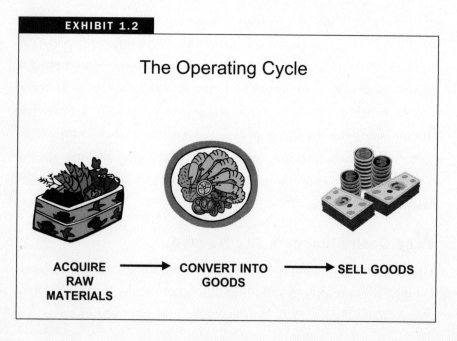

The Operating Cycle

ACQUIRE RAW MATERIALS → CONVERT INTO GOODS → SELL GOODS

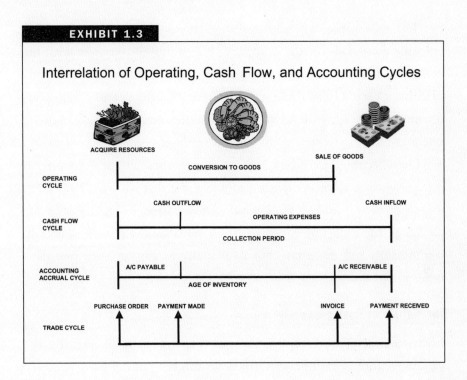

EXHIBIT 1.3

Interrelation of Operating, Cash Flow, and Accounting Cycles

As an example of the preceding, a restaurant buys fresh produce in the morning, transforms the ingredients into meals, which are then sold and paid for during the day. The time between when the cash disbursements are made and the cash is collected is less than a day, that is, the business has an 18–24-hour cash flow cycle.

At the other end of the spectrum, the aircraft industry has a considerably longer operating and cash flow cycle. Years are spent on design and development, and contract negotiations for the purchase of raw materials. This is followed by a protracted manufacturing and testing phase, after which a sale is concluded, usually, on a long-term lease basis.

There are also industries with a reverse cash flow cycle, although these are the exception rather than the rule. For example, in the insurance business, policyholders pay premiums in advance, and claims are paid long after the cash inflow has been received.

The role of the cash manager, in each case, is to ensure that there are sufficient funds for the company to continue in business until the completion of the cash flow cycle. However, each cash manager will perform a very different role, face different challenges, and employ different cash management techniques to assure their company's ongoing operation and liquidity.

Liquidity should not be confused with profitability or net worth. It is possible for a company that is profitable and that has significant assets to go bankrupt from lack of operating (or "working") capital. For example, an airline company can own many valuable assets such as aircraft, landing slots and real estate, but its inability to pay for even one day's fuel can put it out of business.

The Nature of Cash Flows

In managing working capital, the cash manager is challenged by the variable nature of cash flows. Cash flows can be:

- *Mistimed.* Outflows often precede inflows.

- *Mismatched.* Inflows may not entirely cover outflows.

- *Irregular.* Inflows may be uneven. Many seasonal businesses (e.g., retailers and the tourism industry) face extra challenges in managing their cash. Inflows are concentrated during peak months of activity but operating expenses continue throughout the year.

- *Unpredictable.* Cash flows can be difficult to forecast. Bills may be presented earlier than anticipated or the collection of funds may take longer than forecast. The unpredictability factor increases significantly in cross-border business.

The cash manager performs an important role: balancing the company's borrowing and investment activities to maintain the minimum level of liquidity required to sustain the company through the cash cycle.

Positioning the Cash Manager

Although no two companies have identical structures, the cash manager typically reports to the treasurer, who in turn reports to the chief financial officer (CFO) of the company. Exhibit 1.4 shows a representative organization chart.

The CFO is responsible for managing the company's financial position and for quantifying the impact of any capital budgeting or strategic investment decisions being considered. The CFO is usually a member of the senior management team, reporting to the president or chief executive officer (CEO). The major functions that report to the CFO include the treasurer and the comptroller.

- The treasurer will typically be responsible for cash management; overseeing bank relationships, including bank borrowing (short and long term), liquidity management, foreign exchange; risk management; corporate finance; and the management of pension assets.

IN THE REAL WORLD

Centralization of Treasury and Finance

There is no such thing as a "typical" organization. Each company will evolve a structure that is appropriate to its size, business, and priorities. In larger companies, it is usual to see a greater segregation of responsibilities than in smaller companies, where separation of duties is not always economically possible. However, one emerging organizational development that appears to be present in most global companies is the centralization of treasury and finance, to concentrate expertise and bank contact in a single location.

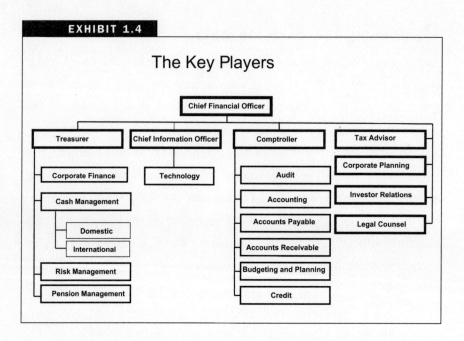

EXHIBIT 1.4

The Key Players

Chief Financial Officer

Treasurer | Chief Information Officer | Comptroller | Tax Advisor

Corporate Finance | Technology | Audit | Corporate Planning

Cash Management | | Accounting | Investor Relations

Domestic | | Accounts Payable | Legal Counsel

International | | Accounts Receivable

Risk Management | | Budgeting and Planning

Pension Management | | Credit

- The comptroller manages the budgeting and planning group, the accounting department, (financial reporting, tax reporting, and internal auditing), and the accounts receivable and accounts payable functions.

The division of labor between the treasurer and the comptroller is important, to ensure that adequate controls are maintained between those who record cash to be disbursed and received and those who actually initiate the movement and receipt of funds.

The cash manager's primary function is to ensure that there are enough *sources* of funds to cover the *uses* of cash required by the company's operating cycle. Sources of funds can be internal, for example, pockets of cash elsewhere in the company, or external, such as from maturing or liquidated investments, borrowing or the sale of assets, goods, or services. The uses of cash include ongoing operating expenses, cost of goods sold, payroll, taxes, repayment of interest or debt, or, in the case of an excess of funds, investments.

The cash manager's time horizon is usually three to six months. Any decisions requiring long-term financing or investment are typically referred to the treasurer level. In order to perform the role effectively, the cash manager has to receive and share information with numerous internal and external sources.

The Role of the Cash Manager

The cash manager's primary day-to-day responsibilities include:

- *Ensuring adequate liquidity.* Maintaining sufficient liquidity reserves to meet the short-term obligations of the company (current liabilities). This requires that sufficient credit is available and that any surplus funds are invested in short-term instruments that can be quickly and easily liquidated.

- *Managing daily cash flows.* Monitoring funds that are received or disbursed, initiating payments and transfers, controlling cash balances in the bank, and moving funds as necessary.

- *Optimizing use of cash resources.* Determining the best use of temporary surplus cash. Leaving balances idle in a disbursement account is not a good use of cash. Assuming that the company is paying a higher rate to borrow than the bank is paying on investments, the best use of funds is to reduce interest expense by repaying debt.

- *Procuring cost-effective financing.* Arranging access to sufficient borrowing capacity, both short- and long-term, in a timely and cost-effective manner. This means that adequate bank relationships are required to assure the necessary levels of funding for the company. The most expensive form of financing is last-minute, unanticipated borrowing.

- *Assessing, monitoring, and controlling risk.* Understanding the nature and scope of financial risks. As companies globalize, the traditional areas of commercial, interest rate, and commodity risk are augmented by foreign exchange and country risks.

The increased use of technology also adds a new kind of risk to be monitored and controlled.

- *Producing timely and accurate short-to-medium-term cash forecasts.* Using forecasting tools to enhance the company's liquidity management, financial control, cost control, and capital budgeting.

- *Managing banking relationships.* Ensuring that the right services are available and are being provided for a "fair" price. This often involves a trade-off between the level of service, timeliness, and cost control.

- *Managing information.* Collecting timely and accurate information. The cash manager is not only dependent upon the inflow of information but is also responsible for coordinating and providing data to other internal sources. The information is crucial for the management of funds, accurate forecasting, updating internal accounting systems, and risk management.

IN THE REAL WORLD

The Changing Role of Banks

The former chairman of Citibank, Walter Wriston, stated that, "Information about money will become more important than the money itself." In today's global economy that was never truer. Unless one is aware that funds are in an account, they may remain idle and unused. The role of the banks in cash management has evolved from primarily processing payments and deposits to being a major provider of information. Increasingly, banks are actively supporting their clients as they move into the world of electronic commerce by sourcing and supplying real-time, detailed, consolidated information.

Important Concepts

The following are six critical concepts in treasury and cash management.

1. *Float.* Float refers to delays in the process of collection, concentration, or disbursement. In the business cycle, float can occur at various points, beginning with the time it takes to issue an invoice and ending when the payer's account is debited. Float is a zero-sum game. Increases in float are to the benefit of the disburser. Conversely, efficiencies in reducing float will be at the cost of the disburser and to the benefit of the person receiving funds. The diagram in Exhibit 1.5 illustrates where float can arise.

   Cash managers spend much of their time managing disbursement and collection float. They are concerned with the float that occurs between the time a payment is due and when the funds become available, if collecting, and the time between when a payment is due and when the funds are debited to the account, if disbursing. Depending on the context and circumstances, every cash manager is both a disburser and a collector of funds. Chapters 3 and 4 on collections and disbursements, respectively, discuss the different types of float and how they are managed.

EXHIBIT 1.5

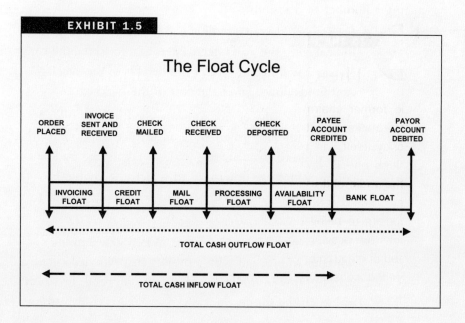

The Float Cycle

ORDER PLACED	INVOICE SENT AND RECEIVED	CHECK MAILED	CHECK RECEIVED	CHECK DEPOSITED	PAYEE ACCOUNT CREDITED	PAYOR ACCOUNT DEBITED
INVOICING FLOAT	CREDIT FLOAT	MAIL FLOAT	PROCESSING FLOAT	AVAILABILITY FLOAT	BANK FLOAT	

TOTAL CASH OUTFLOW FLOAT

TOTAL CASH INFLOW FLOAT

2. *Availability.* Availability refers to the time when funds become usable to the corporate depositor. Depending on the type of instrument being deposited, availability can vary from immediate, as with wire transfers, to two business days for checks issued through U.S. commercial banks distant from where they are deposited. Banks issue complex availability schedules that determine the length of time customers must wait until they can use deposited funds based on the originating point of a check and the drawee bank (see Chapter 3).

3. *Finality.* Finality refers to the point in time at which deposited funds become irrevocable and may not be returned without the prior consent of the beneficiary. For large or urgent transactions, finality is often more important than availability. Wire transfers become available and final upon confirmation of receipt of the wire by the Federal Reserve. Checks may become available but not final until several days later, as they can be debited back to the account if rejected by the drawee bank.

4. *Time value of money.* Time value of money refers to the concept that cash has a higher value if received today rather than tomorrow. Cash that is available today can be invested or used to pay down loans. This concept is important for cash managers in making a number of decisions:

   - *Determining the cost/benefit of a cash management product.* In analyzing the cost effectiveness of a lockbox, the cash manager will need to offset the benefit of the accelerated funds flow against the cost of the lockbox.

   - *Assessing the value of cash discounts.* Vendors may offer a discount for early payment of an invoice. Cash managers need to calculate the value of taking the trade discount against the other uses to which they could be putting the money, or the cost of borrowing money to pay early.

   - *Making capital budgeting decisions.* When determining whether to proceed with a project that will necessitate a cash outflow in the present but that will result in a cash inflow in the future, the cash manager has to determine

TIPS & TECHNIQUES

Reducing Idle Balances

Idle balances are largely the result of the remaining provisions of Regulation Q (see Chapter 8), which prohibits the payment of interest on corporate demand deposits. Cash managers have a number of tools available to reduce idle balances, such as controlled disbursement accounts and sweep accounts. These tools will be discussed in Chapters 3 and 5.

whether the present value of the inflows is greater than the cost of undertaking the project.

- *Investing surplus funds.* When evaluating the returns on different types of investments, the cash manager must be able to bring all of the future returns to a comparable basis before assessing which instrument has the best return.

5. *Opportunity cost.* Opportunity cost is the cost of a foregone alternative use of funds. It is relevant in evaluating a suboptimal situation in comparison to implementing changes toward achieving an ideal solution; for example, attaining the lowest cost in a collection system. Opportunity cost is measured as the cost of the alternative use of funds, such as the lost investment income when idle balances remain in disbursement accounts, or the cost of missed or early payments.

6. *Idle balances.* Idle balances (sometimes referred to as transaction balances) refer to funds that are in a bank account without earning interest. There is an inferred opportunity cost in allowing funds to remain idle.

Summary

In this chapter, we have discussed the major concepts of treasury and cash management and why there is a need for companies to manage their cash efficiently. The chapters that follow will examine the topics of managing corporate cash in more detail.

In addition to the corporate case study that sets the scene for every chapter, the "Tips & Techniques" sections highlight realistic advice for the cash manager. "In the Real World" provides insights into how the theory relates to the actual business world.

The appendices include a list of Web sites of useful sources of information, a suggested reading list with other valuable references, as well as tables of the NACHA formats and SWIFT Message Types most important to the cash manager.

Managing corporate cash is a major challenge for companies and becoming increasingly complex. However, doing it well can have as much impact on company results as a significant new product introduction.

CASE STUDY

As very little has changed over the last 10 years in the way GET-DOE manages its cash, there appear to be many opportunities for significant improvements in the treasury group that will realize some immediate bottom-line efficiencies. Ann will be responsible not only for recommending and implementing the changes, but also for ensuring that Bill and the CFO understand the nature of the innovations and their impact. The CFO comes from the accounting side of the business and, until now, has had no treasury background. Educating the CFO and Bill will be an important part of Ann's role.

CHAPTER 2

Payment Systems

After reading this chapter you will be able to

- Understand the basic terminology used in making payments

- Evaluate the principal U.S. payment methods

- Determine the benefits, costs, and risks associated with each payment method

- Appreciate payment system risk

CASE STUDY

At the request of the treasurer, Bill Fold, Ann I. Shade, the cash manager, is undertaking a complete review of GETDOE's cash management systems. One of the areas that has been highlighted for attention is how the company manages its cash transfers. While many companies in the industry have already moved to electronic payments, GETDOE is still decentralized, hence, disbursements are through many different banks, primarily by check. There has been no opportunity to take advantage of the economies of scale and efficiencies that centralization can provide.

Ann's research revealed that some of the traditional float advantages of paying by check have been eroded by lower interest rates and the collection techniques offered by banks. In addition, the actual cost of issuing and processing checks has been greatly *underestimated, especially when all associated costs are considered, including disbursement equipment, check clearing and reconciliation, and postage. The company is experiencing competitive and supplier pressure to move to electronic payments. Ann and Bill will have to evaluate the implications, trade-offs, and expenses prior to making a decision.*

The U.S. payment system is undergoing a fundamental change. Although still a very heavily paper-dominated system, with checks accounting for nearly 50 billion of the estimated 80 billion payments made annually, a recent study by the Federal Reserve indicates that electronic methods are gaining ground. In the period between 1979 and 2001, even though check volume grew by 55 percent, electronic payments (including credit card transactions) rose from 15 percent up to nearly 40 percent of total volume. Almost 75 percent of electronic payments are made through the ACH. Exhibit 2.1 compares the volumes and value of transactions for 2001 for the major U.S. payment systems.

Important Concepts

In order to understand payment systems, a number of concepts need to be defined.

Clearing and Settlement Systems

Clearing and settlement are two different processes that do not always occur simultaneously or in the same place.

- *Clearing* is the process of recording transactions between members of a clearing channel, such as the Clearing House Interbank Payments System (CHIPS). CHIPS acts as a clearing house for its members but settlement occurs across the members' accounts with the Federal Reserve Bank.

EXHIBIT 2.1

Comparison of U.S. Payment Systems (2001 Annual Volume)

Payment Type	Volume	Value
Fedwire	112.455 million	$423 trillion
CHIPS	60.378 million	$311.7 trillion
ACH	7.994 billion	$22.1 trillion
Checks	49.1 billion	$47.4 trillion

- *Settlement* refers to the act of transferring funds from a payer's account to a beneficiary's account. By definition, settlement can occur only through a bank or between banks. Most often, the central bank in a country acts as the primary settlement agent. Payment systems either settle immediately on a gross basis or after some delay on a net basis. To reduce the risk inherent in delayed settlement, net settlement systems have been shortening the clearing cycle in order to transfer funds closer to the time of origination of the transaction.

Immediate Settlement Systems

The Fedwire, operated by the Federal Reserve System (the Fed), is an example of a real-time gross settlement (RTGS) system. Transactions settle singly or bilaterally with a simultaneous debit to the sender's bank and credit to the receiver's bank. RTGS systems provide same-day finality. They are used for most high-value electronic payment systems because RTGS eliminates many of the intraday and participant settlement risks associated with net settlement.

Delayed Settlement Systems

With a net settlement system (NSS), multiple payments and receipts between participants are settled at the end of a period on a net basis, resulting in a single debit or credit to each member's settlement account. An example is the Automated Clearing House (ACH) that settles one or two business days forward. Due to the delay between initiation and settlement, an intraperiod risk is created. For that reason, NSS systems are usually used for low-value payments.

Hybrid Systems

Increasingly, NSS systems are being redesigned to reduce the time between origination and settlement to reduce risk. There are now a number of systems that settle on a net basis at frequent intervals during the day. Continuous Link Settlement (CLS), discussed in Chapter 7, is an example of a real-time net settlement (RTNS) system.

Transaction Types

There are two primary transaction types:

- *Credit transactions.* The person making the payment (the buyer) initiates a payment transaction to credit the account of a beneficiary.
- *Debit transactions.* The beneficiary initiates a transaction to debit a buyer's account. These transactions are usually preauthorized.

Electronic Payment Methods

U.S. electronic payment systems include Fedwire, CHIPS, and the ACH.

The Fedwire System

Fedwire is an RTGS payment system that processes on a same-day basis without settlement risk to the participants, as the Federal Reserve guarantees payment. It uses a communications system linking the 12 district and 25 branch banks of the Federal Reserve Bank, and is the primary payment system for high-value, domestic U.S. dollars.

Host-to-host computers, online terminals, and other technology link more than 11,000 member institutions. In 2001, the Fed reported that the Fedwire processed an average daily volume of 446,252 transfers, totaling $1.68 trillion, or an average value per transfer of $3.8 million. Participant banks settle through their accounts with the Federal Reserve Bank. Exhibit 2.2 illustrates the payment flow using the Fedwire system.

Fedwire Advantages and Disadvantages

The advantages of using a Fedwire are:

- *Value.* Immediate, same-day value.
- *Settlement.* No settlement risk.
- *Finality.* Funds cannot be recalled without the beneficiary's permission once the payment has been sent by the sending bank and is confirmed by the Federal Reserve Bank.

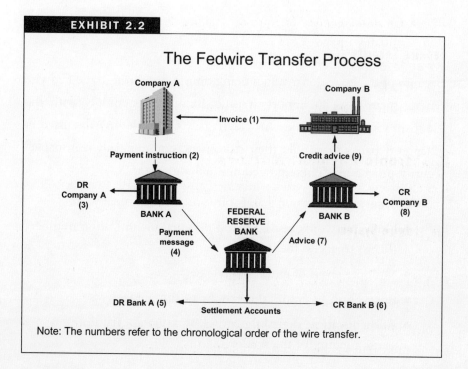

EXHIBIT 2.2

The Fedwire Transfer Process

Note: The numbers refer to the chronological order of the wire transfer.

- *Guaranteed payment.* The Fed guarantees payment should the sending bank fail.
- *Speed.* Very fast, although slight delays may occur when a sending bank has reached its daylight overdraft limit at the Federal Reserve, (see section on payment system risk in this chapter) or at peak operating times, such as when the New York Fed receives the majority of payment instructions.
- *Security.* Reliable and secure.

The major disadvantages are:

- *Cost.* Expensive to use relative to other payment types.
- *Credits only.* Does not process debit transfers.
- *Limited automation linkage.* As not all financial institutions are online with the Fed, some have to make alternative arrangements, either through member banks or over the telephone. This can slow the process and introduce errors.

Fedwire Security

Because of the large dollar values being transferred through the Fedwire system, security is an important issue. In order to comply with the Uniform Commercial Code Article 4A (UCC Article 4A), discussed in Chapter 8, banks must offer their customers "commercially reasonable" security procedures. These procedures include:

- Securing the terminal and software at the company site
- Using passwords, test keys, and personal identification numbers (PINs) to access the system
- Multiple levels of entry and release
- Encryption to ensure the privacy of the message
- Authentication, digital signatures, and digital certificates to assure identity of the sender

- Smart-key devices to secure systems against unauthorized access and use

Fedwire activity continues to grow, in part because the 1980 Monetary Control Act gave increased access to the Fedwire, and in part because of the general growth in business activity. Federal Reserve Bank Fedwire Statistics show that, in 2001, although volume grew by only 3.8 percent the dollar value of transfers grew by 11.6 percent.

In addition to its role in funds transfer, the Fedwire is also used for the settlement of U.S. government securities. Treasury Bills (T-Bills) have been issued in book entry form since 1977. The purchase and sale of these securities occurs by charging and crediting the respective parties' bank accounts by Fedwire.

Clearing House Interbank Payments System (CHIPS)

CHIPS is a bank-owned, computerized telecommunications network operated by the New York Automated Clearing House. It currently links 56 U.S. and foreign banks that have offices in New York City. In 2001, CHIPS processed 95 percent of all international U.S. dollar payments moving among countries. CHIPS handles an average daily volume of 243,500 transactions with a total value of $1.22 trillion, or an average value of $5 million. The majority of the volume comprises interbank movements, Eurodollar payments, and the settling of foreign exchange transactions.

Originally designed as an NSS with settlement at the end of the day, in 2001, CHIPS converted to a real-time net settlement system (RTNS), thereby eliminating most of the daylight overdraft exposure and time delays in effecting payments. The new system also provides enhanced information-reporting capabilities to support the growing e-commerce needs of corporate customers. It can now transmit up to

9,000 characters of data in either standard electronic data interchange (EDI) formats or the new Internet formats, such as Extensible Markup Language (XML).

CHIPS is also used for payments under letters of credit and documentary collections.

CHIPS Advantages and Disadvantages

The advantages of using CHIPS to make payments are:

- *Value.* Immediate, same-day value
- *Settlement.* Settlement risk is virtually eliminated through special prefunded accounts held at the Federal Reserve.
- *Finality.* Funds cannot be recalled after their release into the CHIPS system.
- *Speed.* Very fast, and may be more efficient in using a bank's liquidity than the Fedwire due to the net settlement process
- *Security.* Reliable and secure
- *Information.* Up to 9,000 characters of data can accompany the payment.

The major disadvantages are:

- *Cost.* Expensive to use relative to other payment types, such as ACH
- *Credits only.* Does not process debit transactions
- *Limited direct membership.* Much more limited direct membership than with the Fedwire, although many financial institutions gain access to CHIPS through correspondent relationships with member banks

Automated Clearing House (ACH)

The ACH network offers an electronic alternative to the check. It provides a funds transfer system for U.S. dollar domestic transactions through a network of regional ACHs. The ACH system was established to effect inexpensive settlement of low-value, high-volume, and mainly repetitive payments on a batch basis. According to the National Automated Clearing House Association (NACHA), the annual volume of transactions in 2001 rose to 7.994 billion, representing a total value of $22.1 trillion.

NACHA was established in 1974 to form an interregional link between the ACHs and provide a nationwide electronic payment and collection network among U.S. financial institutions. The characteristics of the ACH are:

- An electronic batch process, store-and-forward system
- Processes both debit and credit transactions
- Transmits additional payment-related information
- Typically used for low value, nonurgent transactions (although the ACH can handle payments of up to $99,999,999.99)
- The type of transaction determines both availability and finality of funds:
    - Credit transactions settle two business days after origination and are final once credited to the beneficiary account.
    - Debit transactions settle one business day after origination and can be refused.
- Originator and receiver settle on the same day, so there is no float associated with ACH payments.

Exhibit 2.3 illustrates the payment flow when a company uses the ACH to pay its employees.

The majority of ACH payments are used for corporate-to-consumer payments. Credit transactions are used for payroll, pension, and annuity payments. Debits transactions, also known as *direct debits,* are used for consumer bill payments, such as utility bills, phone bills, and

EXHIBIT 2.3

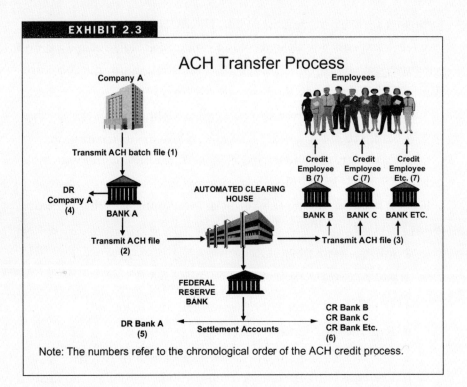

ACH Transfer Process

Note: The numbers refer to the chronological order of the ACH credit process.

insurance premiums. Corporate-to-corporate use has been largely for cash concentration and trade payments.

ACH Advantages and Disadvantages

The advantages of using the ACH to make a payment are:

- *Value.* Payments can be made on precise settlement dates.

- *Cost.* The ACH provides a low-cost, electronic alternative to checks and wires. Current pricing for ACH transactions is in the 10 to 20 cent range, whereas Fedwires can cost more than $10 each for the sender and the recipient.

- *Reliability and efficiency.* Compared with checks, ACH collections are far more predictable.

- *Electronic processing and interfaces.* The system allows for automated interfaces to reconciliation and cash application systems.

- *Payment options.* The ACH handles debit as well as credit transactions, providing opportunities for improved collection processes.

- *Accelerated inflows.* By reducing float in the entire collection process, cash inflows are faster than check receipts.

- *Batch processing.* The ACH handles repetitive batch transactions, such as payroll, pension, and annuity payments (credits), and collection of insurance premiums, utility bills, and mortgage payments (debits).

- *Information.* Large amounts of information can be transferred with the payment.

- *Security.* The system is reliable and secure.

- *Fraud prevention.* While not fraudproof, electronic systems are more secure than paper payments.

The major disadvantages are:

- *Delayed settlement.* ACH payments settle one or two days later than Fedwire and CHIPS payments.

- *Finality.* The ACH does not offer the same guarantee of finality as Fedwire or CHIPS payments, as debits can be returned unpaid.

- *Loss of disbursement float.* ACH transactions clear days faster than checks.

- *Initial start-up costs.* In addition to development and systems costs, there are costs associated with ongoing support and maintenance of dual systems.

- *Change of procedures.* Moving to the ACH requires a change of internal procedures and compliance by customers, vendors, and suppliers.

- *Concerns with debits transactions.* Companies (and consumers) may be unwilling to authorize direct debits to their account due to apprehension concerning security and loss of control. Many banks offer systems that protect against unauthorized debit transactions over preapproved limits.

TIPS & TECHNIQUES

Automated Clearing House Alternative

The majority of payments made by cash managers are known in advance of the due date. Where a specific value date and certainty of settlement are required, such as for contractual payments or debt repayments, the ACH can provide an attractive low-cost alternative to the Fedwire.

- *Uneven capabilities.* Not all financial institutions that claim they are ACH-capable are able to process addenda records.

- *Security.* Controls are not as extensive with the ACH as for Fedwire, making it riskier to use for large-value payments.

Because of the price differential between the Fedwire and the ACH, companies have been increasing their use of the ACH for nonurgent, large-value payments. This is raising concern with the system participants and the regulators about the increased credit risks for the originating depository financial institutions (ODFIs). The risk arises because the ODFI cannot recall or reverse a file once it has been released into the ACH system. With settlement not completed until one or two business days later, the originator may not have sufficient funds in the bank or may have declared bankruptcy. Many banks now require prefunding or a credit facility to be in place to support high-value ACH activity.

Checks

Although the majority of payments in terms of dollar value are completed by electronic means, by far the largest percentage of consumer and corporate payments in terms of volume are made by check, a written order by an account holder to the bank to pay a specified sum of money to the bearer or named recipient. The Depository Financial Institution Check Study found that, in 2001, 49.1 billion checks were written in the United States with a value of $47.4 trillion. The parties in a check transaction are defined as follows:

- The *payor* is the person or company issuing the check.
- The *payee* is the person or company to whom the check is payable.
- The *drawee bank* is the payor's bank on which the check is drawn.
- The *deposit bank* is the financial institution where the payee first deposits the check for crediting to the payee's account.

Characteristics of Checks

Checks are drawn on the payor's demand deposit (checking) account (DDA) at the drawee bank. Negotiability of the document is key to the success of paying with paper instruments. When a check is written, it is made out "Pay to the Order of" the payee, not "Pay to" the payee. This is important in order to enable the check to move through the banking system. The payor allows the drawee bank to pay anyone who presents the item, as long as the payee has signed or endorsed the check. Checks are *demand instruments* and cannot be postdated at the time of presentation to the depository bank.

Traditionally, the check had to move physically from the bank of deposit to the drawee bank. More recently, checks are increasingly being digitized through check truncation and electronic check presentment (ECP). The electronic information is transmitted to the drawee bank and is used for settlement. The check may follow later, be retained by the Federal Reserve or the bank of deposit, or returned to the payor for destruction.

The Check Clearing Process

There are a number of ways in which checks can clear, with most banks using a combination of all methods. Selection of the appropriate method will depend on the deposit bank's availability schedules with various clearing agents, location of the drawee banks, the bank's processing capabilities, and costs (including clearing fees, postage, and couriers). Community and rural banks clear their deposits either through a large correspondent bank or through the Federal Reserve.

The steps in clearing a check are illustrated in Exhibit 2.4. Banks send checks for clearing by means of a *cash letter,* a batch of checks with a tape listing on the cover document that summarizes the content of the bundle and the total dollar value. This cover document acts as a deposit slip for the depositing bank.

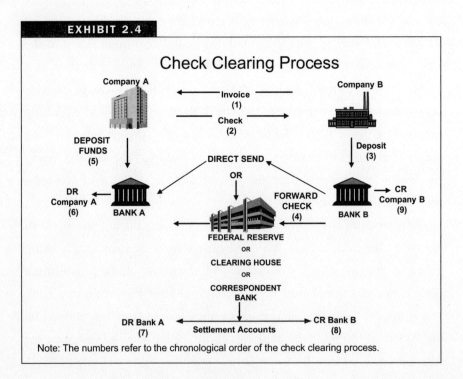

EXHIBIT 2.4

Check Clearing Process

Note: The numbers refer to the chronological order of the check clearing process.

The primary clearing channels are:

- *The Federal Reserve System.* One of the major clearing channels is the Federal Reserve, which operates a nationwide collection facility through its branches and Regional Check Processing Centers (RCPCs). A bank deposits the checks with its local Federal Reserve Bank, which forwards the items to the drawee banks. Once presented, settlement occurs through the banks' settlement accounts with the Fed.

- *Clearing houses.* Many regions operate a local clearing house (i.e., the New York Clearing House Association) to facilitate the exchange of items drawn on member banks. Settlement occurs on a net basis across the accounts maintained with the local Fed.

- *Correspondent banks.* To facilitate business between regions, many banks maintain accounts with other banks (called correspondent banks). The depository bank sends the cash letter to a bank in the area on which the checks are drawn. The use of a correspondent bank network can accelerate availability and reduce the cost of clearing through the Fed.

- *Direct sends.* To achieve faster clearing times, the bank may send the cash letter directly to the drawee bank or distant Fed, if it maintains an account with either. Settlement occurs by crediting the bank of deposit's account with the distant Fed or the correspondent account with the paying bank.

- *On-us clearing.* When the bank of deposit and the paying bank are the same, the bank will make a same-day debit to the payor's account and credit to the payee's account, providing immediate (same-day) availability.

Check Advantages and Disadvantages

The major advantages of using checks are:

- *Readily available.* A checkbook is provided with every demand deposit account. There are no systems to install, training to be given, or education of vendors and suppliers.

- *Widely used.* Checks are widely accepted as a method of payment in the United States.

- *Disbursement float.* The disburser gains float from the delay in mailing payments, processing the items, and check clearing.

- *Efficient.* The check system is well established and the U.S. postal service works efficiently.

- *Limitless information.* When information needs to accompany the payment, it is easy to do so using a remittance document.

- *Anyone, anywhere.* When the details of a payee's bank account are not known, a check can be sent to the address on file.

The major disadvantages are:

- *Fraud.* Paper instruments are much more susceptible to fraud than electronic transfers.

- *Use for international payments.* Checks are not always an acceptable method of payment outside the United States; they can involve a costly collection process, may incur mail delays, and require a currency conversion.

- *Cost.* Due to the ancillary costs of storing, processing, reconciling, and special bank services, such as controlled disbursement and positive pay (described in Chapter 4), the all-in cost of checks can be more expensive than using the ACH.

- *Collection float.* A check delays availability of funds by two or three business days.

- *Finality.* A check can be returned unpaid for a number of reasons, including insufficient funds, a closed account, or a stop-payment order.

Electronic Payments through the ACH

Treasurers who are still using checks extensively should consider converting to electronic payments through the ACH. Disbursement float is diminishing, and the benefits of automated processing in terms of forecasting cash flows, automated reconciliation, cash application, and reduced per-item costs are considerable. Some start-up costs will be incurred, as will renegotiation of contract terms, and education of employees, customers, and suppliers. Most companies, however, find that they can achieve payback within two years.

Other Payment Mechanisms

Although checks are by far the most widely used nonelectronic form of payment, a number of other types of instruments are used in the United States.

Trade Drafts

Trade drafts are primarily used in international transactions, as supported by documentation attesting that the terms of the trade have been met. A draft is a written order to pay, drawn against the payor's bank, and sent through the normal clearing process to the payor's bank by the payee. If a check is an "IOU," then a draft is a "You Owe Me." It is the paper equivalent of a debit transaction through the ACH. The payor retains the right to honor or reject the draft when it is presented to the drawee bank. Drafts can be payable on demand, as with a "sight draft," or at a specified date in the future, called a "time draft."

Bank Drafts (Cashier's Checks)

A bank draft is a check drawn by a bank on its own account. Bank drafts are used in certain transactions where a paper instrument is being presented to close a transaction but the beneficiary requires a bank guarantee of payment. In years past, residential real estate transactions closed with bank drafts; current practice is a wire transfer. Drafts are also used when companies need to make a foreign currency payment but do not maintain an account in that currency. The bank will issue a currency draft drawn on its foreign correspondent bank account.

Cash

A number of businesses remain cash-intensive, such as the fast-food sector of the restaurant industry. Many small retailers with cash sales use these receipts to pay their vendors and employees. This is an efficient use of the cash as it eliminates the cost and time involved in making cash deposits. For other types of businesses, however, while cash provides the illusion of instantaneous availability, unless it is going to be used for disbursing, cash has little value until it has been deposited into a bank account.

The advantages to using cash are:

- *Fungible.* Small amounts of cash are nearly always accepted.
- *Speed and finality.* Funds are assured as soon as cash changes hands.

The disadvantages to using cash are:

- *Physical nature.* Cash has to be physically handled, and, if lost, cannot be replaced.
- *Low dollar value.* It is usually not acceptable for large dollar transactions.
- *Fraud.* Modern technology enables currency notes to be very convincingly reproduced. Machines for detecting fraudulent

bills are available, but counterfeiting continues to be a major problem.

- *Nonearning asset.* Cash is a nonearning asset until deposited or used.

- *Security.* Extra security and costs may be involved in transporting cash to the point of deposit.

- *Audit trail.* Cash provides no audit trail, and, therefore, cash-intensive businesses are often targeted by the Internal Revenue Service.

The nontraceable nature of cash also makes it especially suspect when traded in large quantities. Money laundering is a major concern in the United States and banks must complete a Currency Transaction Report (CTR) for all deposits of $10,000 or more, even for interbank transactions.

Credit and Charge Cards

Credit and charge cards (also referred to collectively as plastic) allow the vendor to receive value on a transaction while the purchaser enjoys a grace period of up to 30 days before the bill is presented. Companies use a number of different types of plastic card.

- With *charge cards,* such as American Express, the full amount is due when the bill is presented. There is often no preset spending limit and the issuing company charges an annual fee to the cardholder.

- With *credit cards,* such as MasterCard and Visa, a minimum payment is due upon presentment of the bill, but the remaining balance can be paid over a period of time, thereby extending credit. Credit cards have a stated purchasing limit, and interest rates on the unpaid balance are at the top end of the legal limits. Credit cards are usually one of the most expensive sources of credit.

- With *corporate charge cards* companies issue cards to employees who are authorized to make purchases on the company's behalf. The bill is presented to the employee, who is responsible for paying the amount in full. The employee then reclaims the expenses through the company's reimbursement process.

Procurement Cards

More recently, many companies have started using procurement cards, also known as purchasing cards, to reduce the costs and related administration of purchasing within the company. Unlike the corporate charge card, the card issuer sends the consolidated, detailed invoice of all of the purchases for the billing period directly to the company for payment. The company pays with a single payment. The details are available electronically to enable the company to update its records and automatically reconcile the accounting for purchases. Procurement cards are discussed in more detail in Chapter 4.

Payment System Standardization

Payment system efficiencies depend upon the standardization of messages that are used to transmit information between trading partners and banks. The following are the major initiatives to standardize payment system formats.

Electronic Data Interchange (EDI)

Electronic data interchange refers to the electronic exchange of information between trading partners using formatted messages. EDI allows companies to initiate messages directly from their internal applications to be communicated electronically to the receiving party. EDI standards were developed in the early 1980s by dominant companies (such as General Motors) for use with their own trading partners. Industries such as chemicals, oil, transportation, and medical services all have developed conventions and message formats for use when trading between buyers and sellers.

Financial Electronic Data Interchange (FEDI) refers to EDI messages concerning financial transactions, such as lockbox reports, the account analysis, remittance advices, and payment initiation. Many FEDI message types use NACHA or Accredited Standards Committee (ASC) X12 formats. EDIFACT, the EDI standard in development by the United Nations, is widely used in Europe.

Although EDI had been used initially to digitize the communication process, more recent developments have enabled companies to also reengineer the business cycle to make it more efficient. Examples of applications that streamline the value chain by eliminating both the order and invoicing processes include:

- *Paid-on-Production* (POP), where payment for goods becomes due and is automatically generated upon use in the manufacturing process.

IN THE REAL WORLD

EDI Outside
the United States

The United States has led the way in the development and use of EDI, largely due to the leverage of some of the world's biggest multinational companies. As a result, EDI has been adopted as standard operating practice by a number of industries. Outside of the United States, adoption has been slower, due to the perceived high cost of entry in terms of systems, technology interfaces, and trading partner resistance. Many smaller companies that are not already involved in using EDI see the development of Web-based applications as a low-cost way of achieving the same levels of automation and end-to-end processing efficiencies.

- *Evaluated Receipts Settlement* (ERS), when a restocking message is electronically initiated and a payment is made based on the receipts at the loading dock.

NACHA Formats

NACHA has developed a number of formats to handle ACH transactions. These standardized messages are used by all banks and parties involved in originating, processing, and receiving ACH payments. Appendix B lists some of the formats most commonly used by cash managers, such as the cash concentration or disbursement (CCD) format for cash concentration.

SWIFT

The Society for Worldwide Interbank Financial Telecommunications (SWIFT) is a bank-owned, global telecommunications system. Developed in the early 1970s, it created a series of strictly standardized messages for the exchange of financial information between financial institutions. Electronic links have been built between SWIFT and the local electronic clearing systems in many countries, allowing messages to pass through in an entirely automated fashion. For example, CHIPS members in New York who need to send an international wire transfer have a direct link between their back-office system, the CHIPS system, and SWIFT. This allows a formatted message to pass straight-through, electronically from originator to recipient, to the clearing house and settlement bank.

Most recently, SWIFT has moved into creating formatted messages for other financial players and new mediums, such as transferring the entire letter of credit process onto the Internet and providing Web-based functionality for business-to-business (B2B) transactions with SWIFTNet. Appendix C provides a chart of the SWIFT message types that are of most interest to cash managers, such as the MT 100 message series, used for money transfers, and the MT 900 series, used for balance reporting.

Payment System Risk

For the last two decades, the Federal Reserve has been concerned with the possibility of the failure of one or more large financial institutions. Measures have been introduced by the Fed to reduce payment system risk by assuring the finality of payment.

Daylight overdrafts (when an account is overdrawn at the Fed during the course of the day) are a particular concern, as this situation creates an intraday credit exposure. To control the level of daylight overdrafts, the Fed requires that all banks put in place a *sender net debit cap,* limiting the intraday overdraft that a bank may incur across all the large dollar payment systems. The Fed also has the right to charge banks for any daylight overdraft at their Fed account.

Most recently, the ACH moved to bring the times of settlement and finality for ACH credits closer together. Under the previous policy, the Fed had the right to reverse a transaction up to 24 hours after settlement. The new policy, "ACH Settlement Day Finality," effective June 2001, means that credit originations become final at the same time as they post, at 8.30 A.M. ET on settlement day. However, in order to achieve this, the Fed requires that any forward ACH credit transactions be prefunded at the Fed settlement account.

Summary

This chapter reviewed and compared the major payment vehicles used in the United States, along with their advantages and disadvantages. It discussed the different types of clearing channels and the mechanisms that can render the systems more efficient. The following chapters will look in more detail as to how these payment systems are used in the collection, concentration, and disbursement processes, and the implications of each for the cash manager.

CASE STUDY

After consideration of the advantages and disadvantages of electronic payments, Ann has determined that GETDOE should begin to migrate its disbursements to the ACH. She fears that if the necessary changes are not initiated, GETDOE will eventually lose competitive advantage by not being as efficient as its peers in the industry. Ann realizes that the process will not be accomplished overnight and that much negotiation lies ahead with GETDOE's employees, vendors, and suppliers.

CHAPTER 3

Managing Cash Inflows

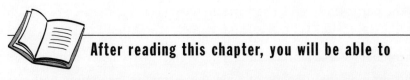

After reading this chapter, you will be able to

- Understand the design of a collection system, given the constraints of the banking system

- Appreciate the reasons for the dominance of paper transactions

- Review internal techniques and bank products used to manage collection float

- Learn about ancillary collection activities

CASE STUDY

Bill Fold's cash manager, Ann I. Shade, is responsible for managing GETDOE's bank accounts, including the movement of funds between banks. Bill has been complaining that there are too many accounts, now numbering 65, with one or two at each office, factory, or distribution center. The accounts are used to deposit funds received from the invoicing-receivables cycle at each location. The administrative time and banking costs are significant, and it isn't certain that funds received are deposited in a timely manner.

Bill and Ann have attended meetings of the local cash management association to learn more about the lockboxing systems used by other companies. One treasurer explained that he was able to reduce his collection banks to two accounts: one lockbox DDA and one regular DDA. This change resulted in significant savings in time, banking costs, and administration. Bill and Ann are considering how GETDOE can also realize similar efficiencies.

The purpose of a collection system is to accelerate the receipt of cash inflows from customers, subsidiaries, and other parties that owe money to the corporation. The events that trigger cash inflows occur through the timeline of collection activities, beginning with the initial sale of product and continuing through invoicing, the receipt of funds, and the depositing of those funds in a commercial bank. This chapter reviews the traditional cash management concerns of mail, processing, and availability float for payments made by paper check.

Inefficiencies in Collection Activities

A principal reason that inefficiencies occur in treasury management is *float,* which is often defined as funds in the process of collection, disbursement, or other movement. Float exists in the United States largely because of our legislative history—the McFadden Act (1927) and the Glass-Steagall Act (1933) required the establishment of separate financial institutions in each state and each financial services industry (see the discussion of the relevant laws in Chapter 8).

McFadden and Glass-Steagall were effectively repealed in the 1990s by the Interstate Banking and Branching Efficiency Act (1994) and the Gramm–Leach–Bliley Act (1999). Nevertheless, the number of commercial banks is still in excess of 8,000. This requires the movement of physical checks between the payor and the payee, and the drawee and deposit banks, causing a delay in the receipt of "good," or collected, funds by the depositor.

The Role of Paper

Despite efforts to convert remittances by check to electronic mechanisms, the United States is writing about 50 billion checks each year. Checks are the prevalent payment mechanism for several reasons:

- Payment convenience
- Evidence of the remittance and long-established in law
- Accepted by most businesses
- Float management for the remitter
- Low banking cost (although the all-in cost can be expensive)
- An efficient process

Other forms of collection float occur earlier in the timeline activities before the check enters the U.S. Postal System (USPS). These float components are often managed by business units, information technology, or accounts receivable, not by treasury. The focus of this chapter will be on the elements under the control of treasury—mail, processing, and availability float. Collections float may involve several days, and is composed of three components:

1. *Mail float.* The time between the mailing of a check and the arrival at its destination
2. *Processing float.* The time between the receipt of the check and its deposit in a financial institution
3. *Availability float.* The time between the depositing of the check and the corporation's access to "good" funds

See Exhibit 3.1 for a graphical presentation of these float elements.

Mail Float

It may appear that there is little a recipient can do to reduce mail float because of the complete control of mail delivery by the USPS. In fact, the location of the sites to which the USPS delivers may significantly affect mail time.

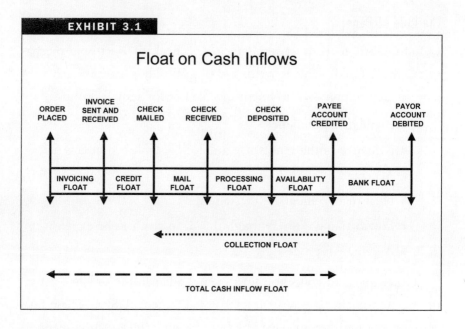

EXHIBIT 3.1

Float on Cash Inflows

| ORDER PLACED | INVOICE SENT AND RECEIVED | CHECK MAILED | CHECK RECEIVED | CHECK DEPOSITED | PAYEE ACCOUNT CREDITED | PAYOR ACCOUNT DEBITED |

| INVOICING FLOAT | CREDIT FLOAT | MAIL FLOAT | PROCESSING FLOAT | AVAILABILITY FLOAT | BANK FLOAT |

COLLECTION FLOAT

TOTAL CASH INFLOW FLOAT

Causes of Mail Float

Many businesses receive mail at one or more office locations, and a first step in evaluating improvement opportunities is to determine whether these sites are optimal. As a rule, city locations are faster than suburban or rural post offices, because most mail is sorted in main postal facilities and then delivered to secondary centers.

The fastest mail cities in the United States currently are Chicago and Atlanta, where mail is available at the main post offices as early as 5:00 A.M. Mail for the suburbs of Chicago or Atlanta and rural Illinois or Georgia (or for any noncity location) must then be transferred to those locations for delivery to postal customers. The difference between Chicago/Atlanta city mail times and the suburbs can be as much as one-third business day (or about two and a half hours), which can impact an entire day's cash processing activity.

To see how this can occur, assume that a company is located in a suburban office park where it receives its mail by USPS delivery at

46

11:00 A.M. The sorting and opening of the mail requires another hour, or until noon, the customary lunch hour. When the clerical staff returns at 1:00 P.M., it may spend another two hours to complete the accounting for the cash that has been received (the cash application process), prepare the deposit ticket, endorse the checks, and get a deposit ready for transmittal to the bank (the cashiering process).

Now it's 3:00 P.M., and an employee (or private messenger) takes the deposit to the local bank branch, which closes at 4:00 P.M. However, the deposit will not receive credit at the bank until tomorrow, because the branch has a 2:00 P.M. deposit cut-off time. This is because the bank's courier—who comes by once a day—stops by at 2:30 P.M. on the way to the other branches and eventually to the main processing center, and the tellers need about 30 minutes to prepare the package of check deposits.

Solutions to Mail Float

The *one-third day longer* mail delivery time has an economic cost to a company of an *entire day* in starting the collection float process. In determining whether one day matters, assume that a company receives $250 million a year in mailed payments, or $1 million each business day. If the cost of funds (discussed in Chapter 9) is a conservative 10 percent, the delay of a day is worth an annual $100,000! Several actions can be taken to reduce this cost.

Mail can be directed to a post office box in the main processing facility servicing a metropolitan area. A courier service can be arranged to pick up the mail beginning early in the morning, bring it to the company's offices, and have it sorted and ready for work when employees arrive at 8:00 A.M. If there is a sufficient quantity of mail, the courier can make a second run to the post office at about 8:30 A.M., when all incoming items should be available for distribution.

Alternatively, a post office box can be established at a nearby postal facility, but the mail will not likely be sorted and ready for distribution until about 10:00 A.M. The additional two hours may be critical to the completion of the cash deposit. Finally, the deposit can be taken directly to the bank's operations center, where the deposit time for credit today may be as late as 5:00 or 6:00 P.M. The manager's goal is to make the bank deposit in time to receive credit for today, not tomorrow.

Processing Float

The goal of managing processing float is to require zero days; that is, to deposit all items on the same day they are received. Unfortunately, many businesses hold on to checks received until the end of the processing cycle. Typically, the mailroom passes along envelopes with remittances to accounts receivable, where there may be two or three workstations with responsibility for recording payments against open invoices, noting any disputes, and following up with customers. The payment then goes to treasury, where the cashier creates the deposit ticket, endorses each check, and prepares a package for the trip to the bank.

Depending on the complexity of a company's receivables and cashiering cycle, processing float may take as much as one week. In other situations, employees simply hold on to checks until they remember to take them to the cashier. If the employee usually works out of the office, checks may be turned in only once or twice a week, on the days

---

TIPS & TECHNIQUES

Same-Day Credit

A simple way to determine if a company is receiving same-day credit for its deposits is to compare the dates on the bank statement to those on the daily deposit tickets. If the dates are consistently one business day off, deposits are arriving too late for that day's ledger credit.

when other matters require an office visit. The same calculation from the discussion of mail float applies here: If an item is held even one extra day, a $250-million business loses $100,000 a year.

Availability Float

The development of the U.S. banking system has been constrained by federal legislation limiting banks to doing business in the states in which

TIPS & TECHNIQUES

Solution to Processing Float

One possible solution to the processing float problem is to send all envelopes likely to contain remittances directly to the cashiering area. To expedite the separation of general mail and envelopes containing remittances, a special internal mail code can be incorporated into the address, such as Department 321. The cashier can pull all checks, make copies, and send the material on to receivables for cash application. Meanwhile, the checks can be taken to the bank with the minimum of delay.

There are two informal ways to determine the extent of any processing float in a company:

 After everyone has gone home at the end of the day, go through the desks of receivables staff and other relevant functions. Processing float is a problem if any significant volume of checks is found sitting in piles with remittance documents, awaiting processing.

 Going through employees' desks makes most managers understandably squeamish. An alternative approach is to instruct the mailroom to open all envelopes and keep a log of any with checks, then compare the deposit date for each check against the date the mailroom received the item.

IN THE REAL WORLD

One Company's Results

One large financial services company tried both approaches, and found to its dismay that processing float averaged four business days. The principal reason: The company had a 24-hour turn-around rule for file processing at each workstation, but there were an average of five separate operations before cash was ready to go to the bank.

they were initially chartered. We discuss this issue in Chapter 8. The result of this restriction was the requirement for depositories to physically present checks to the banks on which they were drawn.

For example, a company with offices in Arizona most likely uses a local bank for its deposits. However, the checks it receives may be drawn on banks in New England or states in the Southeast, some 3,500 miles distant. The depositor must await the transportation of the checks back to the East Coast to receive credit for the deposit.

Internal Bank Deadlines

In order to assess when balances become available, several critical times during the banking day must be considered.

- The *deposit deadline,* which specifies the time in the bank's day by which a company must make a deposit for it to be included in that day's work. Deadlines vary within each bank; for example, a deposit made at a branch must be made significantly earlier than a deposit taken to the bank's processing center.

- The *ledger cut-off time,* at which time the bank stops processing work for that business day and begins its next working day. For example, a ledger cut-off of 2:00 P.M. means that at 2:01

P.M. the bank begins the following business workday. Depositing an item on Tuesday at 3:00 P.M. means that it will be considered a deposit on Wednesday. If the deposit deadline is 2.30 P.M., the deposit will need to be made before 2.30 P.M. on Monday in order to be part of the bank's work for Tuesday (i.e., between 2:01 P.M. Monday and 2:00 P.M. on Tuesday).

- The *availability schedule* specifies the number of days or fractions of a day the depositor will have to wait before the bank will grant availability, or the funds are considered as collected. In the United States, availability float is usually between zero and two business days. The different availability assignments are based on how the check moves through the clearing system. On-us checks—those deposited in the bank on which they were drawn—and U.S. Treasury checks receive zero or same-day credit, as do Fedwire transfers. Checks drawn on local and regional banks and on banks in major cities receive one or next-day credit, as do ACH transfers. Distant points require two business days. (Clearing alternatives are discussed in Chapter 2.)

Bank Processing

The bank reads the information from the bottom of the check—the magnetic ink character recognition (MICR) line—to know how to route the check back to the drawee bank. Exhibit 3.2 provides a schematic view of a check, with particular emphasis on the MICR line.

The significant MICR fields include:

- The *transit routing number* (TRN), sometimes called the ABA number. This nine-digit address contains four subfields:

  1. The first two digits indicate the Federal Reserve District of the drawee bank.

  2. The second two digits indicate whether the bank is in a city location, regional check processing center (RCPC), or country (rural) bank.

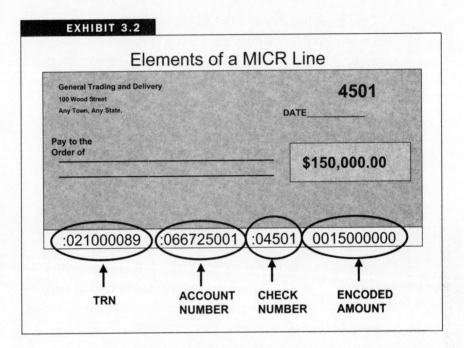

EXHIBIT 3.2

Elements of a MICR Line

General Trading and Delivery
100 Wood Street
Any Town, Any State,

4501

DATE_____

Pay to the
Order of
_____

$150,000.00

:021000089 :066725001 :04501 0015000000

TRN ACCOUNT NUMBER CHECK NUMBER ENCODED AMOUNT

3. The next four digits comprise the bank-specific number, usually assigned in the sequence that the bank was federally chartered.

4. The last digit is a check verification digit, used in determining the integrity of the TRN.

For example, a check written on Citibank in New York City has a TRN of 0210 0008 9: "02" is the second Federal Reserve District; "10" is a city designation; "0008" is the number assigned to the bank; and "09" is the check (or verification) digit.

- The account number assigned by the bank to its customer.

- The check number assigned when the check is printed. We will see in Chapter 4 that checks can be created entirely on a single print run, eliminating the requirement for preprinted check stock.

- The dollar amount of the check. The encoding of this amount can occur in three ways:

1. The company can encode the dollar amount of the check when the deposit is being prepared. Check encoders are commercially available for a few hundred dollars.

2. The bank where the check is deposited can encode the check. Although this is the easiest approach, the bank will charge about 2 cents per check if an item is "unencoded," and will require the deposit at the bank two hours before the announced close of "ledger" credit.

3. The dollar amount can be encoded when the issuing company prints the face of the check.

Solutions for Availability Float

While a manager could attempt to compare bank availabilities, there is usually very little difference due to bank competition in the assignment process. The availability received can be improved by locating the deposit account near or at the bank on which the largest dollar amount of checks received are drawn. In order to do the analysis, remittances for the past month (or other representative period) are reviewed to determine the drawee banks used by major customers. There are two problems with this strategy:

 TIPS & TECHNIQUES

Electronic Fund Transfers

The active conversion of customer payments from paper check to electronic funds transfers (wires or ACH) is one way to reduce mail, processing, and availability float. (Electronic payment mechanisms were discussed in Chapter 2). Experience varies by industry in promoting the use of EFT, and often requires some inducement. Examples include lower mortgage rates for customers agreeing to pay by ACH, or requiring monthly insurance payments by ACH debit.

1. Numerous accounts may be required to deposit these various checks, which may not be cost-effective.

2. Some of these banks may be hundreds or thousands of miles from the company's offices, making it impractical to travel to these locations every time the company receives a large check.

Lockboxing

After the Second World War, banks realized that there might be a business opportunity in helping companies to manage their collection float. The concept of lockboxing was developed to reduce corporate client involvement in the handling of incoming checks. Lockbox services comprise several interrelated services:

- Receive mail in a bank-controlled post office box in the city/cities of their major processing centers.

- Pick up mail numerous times each day beginning at about 5:00 A.M.

- Bring mail back to the bank processing site.

- Open mail.

- Determine if any checks received should not be deposited based on instructions from the company (such as the wrong payee or a post-dated payment).

- Take a copy or image of checks approved for deposit.

- Deposit acceptable checks that have been received.

- Assign availability and clear deposited checks.

- Send electronic information about the remittances to the company (followed by physical copies of the checks, undeposited checks, and the remittance documents).

The lockbox product quickly became successful because, for a relatively nominal cost, companies were relieved of the burden and delay of handling mail and check deposits. The popularity of this service led to its being offered by the largest 100 or so banks throughout the United

States. Until about 1985, each bank limited its lockbox services to the state in which it was domiciled, largely because of restrictions on out-of-state banking. This forced companies to open several lockboxes to provide geographic coverage for their customer remittances. The resulting system was expensive, somewhat difficult to manage, and required the subsequent concentration of funds to a central bank account so that funds could be invested, disbursed for expenses, or used to pay down loans. (See Chapter 4 on concentration banking).

To assist with the determination of lockbox cities and banks, a collection model was developed by Phoenix-Hecht, a financial marketing research firm located in Research Triangle Park, North Carolina. Banks subscribe to the model and the accompanying databases of mail and availability times, and they offer to perform float studies for their corporate clients for a small fee. The model determines the optimal locations based on a representative sample of checks received and the senders' envelopes, using such data as the TRN, the postmark date, and the sending zip code.

Lockbox Networks

By the late 1980s, several of the largest financial institutions organized lockbox networks to provide a nationwide service to their clients. Exhibit 3.3 lists lockbox networks.

A single bank can now offer lockbox services in each region of the country; for example, Mellon Bank offers sites in Pittsburgh, its home city, and in Atlanta, Boston, Chicago, Dallas, Los Angeles, and Philadelphia. The corporate customer can use any or all of these sites, managed by one bank through one bank account, while achieving national coverage in the major business cities. The banks were able to circumvent interstate banking restrictions by establishing processing sites outside of their state of domicile, using a local bank for the actual check deposit and clearing process.

EXHIBIT 3.3

Lockbox Networks

Bank of America	PNC
Bank One	Regulus Group
J.P. Morgan Chase	Wachovia
Mellon	Wells Fargo

Source: Phoenix-Hecht 2001 Cash Management Monitor

As the number of lockbox banks required began to decline due to the networks, companies saw no reason to continue with multibank cash management systems. It became easier to use one bank for all collection/ concentration activity, and to use that same bank for any disbursement services required (see Chapter 4). This trend toward the consolidation of company collection sites has been precipitated by lockbox profitability problems and the required investment in new technologies, primarily imaging. These developments are reviewed in later sections of this chapter.

TIPS & TECHNIQUES

Complimentary Float Studies

Banks offering lockbox networks will often conduct complimentary float studies to determine the best configuration for prospective clients. However, they typically confine potential solutions to their sites, excluding sites not served by their network. It is important to implement a lockbox only at those sites recommended in the analysis, because each site added to the solution can incur an additional monthly fixed charge of $100 to $150.

Wholesale Lockbox

The original form of lockbox services—now commonly known as *wholesale lockbox*—was established to handle low-volume, high-dollar checks. Critical data fields are manually key-entered from the remittance document, such as the customer and/or invoice number, while check MICR data is captured in an automated flow as the documents pass through the bank's reader-sorters. This process works effectively when there are a limited number of standard remittance documents and when an invoice copy is returned with the check. The bank can review its operating instructions and templates for the account, determine which data to key, and complete the transaction.

TIPS & TECHNIQUES

Customizing Remittance Documents

One way to minimize wholesale lockbox problems is to review all remittance documents used for customer billing. A standard, understandable invoice should be used, with the only printed address being that of the lockbox. A company telephone number and Internet address should be provided for questions and customer service, but no company address should be indicated. Include a return envelope for customer convenience, and make certain that the size of the remittance document and envelope match so that paper folds won't occur over scan lines or barcodes.

Too many companies clutter their invoice packages, making them nearly indecipherable. The problem is compounded by the issuance of monthly statements, dunning letters requesting payment, and other correspondence. Make it as easy as possible for customers to pay; a commercial graphic designer can help.

Customers that do not return remittance documents, or situations when banks receive multiple types of invoices, are a chronic problem for lockbox clerks and the company. Most companies instruct their banks to deposit all checks received, including those lacking adequate support detail. The company is then forced to work from the check copy and any other evidence, including the customer's envelope and accompanying correspondence, to apply cash, move the cash item from suspense, and close the receivable.

Ancillary Collection Services

Various other collection services supplement wholesale lockbox, and must be considered by any company reviewing its cash management system.

Retail Lockbox

Some banks offer a totally electronic data capture environment, usually referred to as *retail lockbox*. Processing equipment scans the MICR line on checks and the optical character recognition (OCR) line on remittance documents, automatically providing lockbox detail. Because there is minimal operator intervention, the workflow is efficient and inexpensive. (OCR is an alternative technology for automated character scanning that is often used on retail invoices.)

Banks have found it difficult to make their target profitability returns on retail lockbox, due to the extensive investment in equipment and the low price that is typically charged for the service. As a result, many banks no longer offer retail lockbox. Companies have the option of using the services of specialized retail processing vendors such as EDS, GTE Processing, and NPC. Although the vendor deposits processed checks at a local bank, there is some exposure to the company during the intraday period before the bank receives the deposit.

Imaging

Imaging is a technology that permits the digitized scanning, sorting, cataloging, and retrieval of paper documents, including checks, remittances, envelopes, and correspondence. Several banks acquired imaging equipment for a few selected uses, including various disbursement services (see Chapter 4), and have extended the technology to such other applications as lockbox. Images can replace the labor-intensive process of handling wholesale lockbox items, while increasing the flexibility of the data captured and the scope and speed of receivables information transmitted to the company.

The process requires the company to establish a template of standard invoices used in billing customers. The typical imaging workflow scans incoming items, searches for relevant data fields in specific areas of the invoice and check, captures those data, and creates a file for transmission to the company. Same-day information is sent by various transmittal methods, including T-1 (dedicated) telecommunications lines or through the bank's Web site. Companies that can await more infrequent transmittals may choose to receive images on weekly or biweekly CD-ROMs.

Integrated Receivables

Some banks offer a single entry point for all incoming receipts in payment of open receivables. Variously known as *comprehensive receivables* or *electronic lockbox,* integrated receivables accommodates any type of electronic or paper transaction. The lockbox merges receipt data into a single file transmission to the company, eliminating the need to manage multiple cash and data flows.

Other Services

All collection items must be deposited in a checking or demand deposit account (DDA), for which banks charge a maintenance fee and per-item charges such as deposit tickets processed and checks deposited. Other required services may include the processing and vaulting of incoming coin and currency, the replenishment of coin and currency at cashiering locations, and armored car cash pickup or drop-off. Companies accepting credit or debit cards typically pay financial institutions a fee of 1.5 to 2.5 percent for processing these transactions.

Pricing

Except for imaging, all of the collection products discussed in this chapter are very mature, with competitive pricing by financial institutions. (For comparative prices of these and other cash management services, see the Executive Summary of the *Blue Book of Bank Prices* on the Phoenix-Hecht Web site, *www.phoenixhecht.com.*)

In evaluating listed prices, it is important to note that prices are unbundled, that is, each component of a service is separately itemized on the bank's invoice or account analysis. For example, the *Blue Book* separately prices the wholesale lockbox processing charge (currently averaging 43 cents) and the check copy charge (currently 11 cents). Each service can have as many as six to eight separate components, including fixed charges not based on the number of items processed. The current *Blue Book* monthly wholesale lockbox fixed charge is $110, to which would normally be added various other unit charges based on activity volume.

Typical pricing is provided in Exhibit 3.4. The charges listed are aggregated, and include the components typically used by most corporations; see Exhibit 3.5.

Banks discount pricing based almost entirely on volume, with 20,000 or more items a month usually required for a reduction of their charges. That said, it is generally inadvisable to focus entirely on the cost of a service. Any service or quality problems will cost far more to resolve than the few cents of savings that may be attained through hard negotiation. Furthermore, the trend toward the consolidation of bank relationships (discussed in Chapter 9) will force companies to award their

EXHIBIT 3.4

Typical Pricing of Collection Services

Service	Aggregated Price Per Item*
Internal processing of cash receipts	varies: typically $1–$3
Wholesale Lockbox	60 cents
Retail Lockbox	25 cents
Depository Services	25 cents (including deposit ticket)
Coin and Currency	coin: 12 cents; currency: 60 cents

*Excluding fixed charges such as account maintenance

cash management business to one or a few banks, reducing the possibility of extensive price comparisons.

Other Considerations

Lockbox is a long-established product with proven success in addressing several concerns faced by business:

- Reducing internal costs and collection float
- Avoiding the risk of fraud by having a bank handle incoming checks
- Simplifying the collection workflow with minimum cost and effort
- Speeding access to current payment information for customers on a "credit watch"

However, there are issues to consider in evaluating any such change to a collection system.

EXHIBIT 3.5

Components of Paper-Based Collection Services

Credit posting	Branch deposits
Lockbox maintenance*	Branch furnished coin and currency
Lockbox item processing	Unencoded checks (pricing varies by drawee location)
Lockbox photocopy	
Lockbox data capture: OCR/MICR	Return item processing
Lockbox data capture: alphanumeric	Deposit reconciliation maintenance*
Lockbox exceptions	Deposit reconciliation processing

*Fixed charges not based on item volume

Operational Control of Collections

A number of large organizations allow operational areas rather than treasury to manage their collection activities. Evidence of this situation would be if treasury staff is uncertain as to the purpose of a particular lockbox (or bank account), or if it is not known who selected current banks or city sites, or if payment technology (i.e., credit/debit cards) is being considered but no one has informed treasury. In these cases, the likelihood is that business units (and not treasury) made the decision, and financial management has been excluded from all consideration but the compensation to the bank.

Lockbox Holdover

Bankers assure their customers that incoming lockbox mail is processed in the early-morning hours to make important availability times (i.e., at 5:00 A.M.). However, quite often, a portion of remittances at some lockbox banks is received in the late morning and early afternoon. This results in deposits after the cut-off time for ledger credit, and the loss of a day's availability.

Remitter Cooperation

Any lockbox application requires the cooperation of remitting organizations; that is, they must mail their payment to the special bank address (usually a post office box) specified on the invoice. The change to a lockbox address is obvious to any business manager, and attempts to extend float may be made by their insistence on mailing to the corporate address. This refusal may also result from their failure to change the file address. In any event, pursuit and constant written reminders may be necessary to have mail properly directed to the bank's facility.

Summary

The preeminent role of paper in the U.S. business system has led to the development of various internal and banking procedures to manage collections. Float cannot be eliminated so long as consumers and businesses pay by check. It is important, therefore, to implement techniques to minimize the time to "good" funds, including lockboxing and efficient post office and cashiering procedures.

CASE STUDY

Bill and Ann reviewed their current collection system, and decided that the $120 million in annual check receipts (representing about 6,000 items) could be managed more efficiently by a bank lockbox network. With assistance from their bankers, they calculated that about three days of total float would be saved, worth $100,000 ($120 million/360 calendar days × 3 days × 10 percent cost of funds).

In addition, they would be able to close many of their bank accounts, greatly reduce administrative time, and avoid moving funds between accounts or leave idle balances in their banks. The cost of the lockbox arrangement would be about $6,000 (6,000 items × 60 cents + $200/month in account maintenance and other fixed charges). With the closing of the bank accounts and the elimination of balances and funds movement, the total savings developed were well in excess of $100,000 a year.

CHAPTER 4

Managing Cash Outflows

After reading this chapter, you will be able to

- Review how funds in depository and lockbox accounts are mobilized through the process of cash concentration

- Understand disbursement system approaches to sending payments to vendors, employees, and others with the appropriate timing, cost, and mechanism

- Evaluate controls against fraud and other criminal activities in paper-based disbursement systems

- Learn of new approaches to purchasing and accounts payable cycles

CASE STUDY

The lockbox system that was implemented was so successful that Bill Fold wonders if changes should be made to the company's concentration and disbursement systems, also managed by Ann I. Shade. Bill is particularly concerned about the external CPA's recent audit comment regarding the national increase in check fraud and potential problems with the disbursement systems used by GETDOE. In addition, he wonders if there are any possible cost or float savings worth investigating, and if centralizing disbursements might make the entire process more efficient.

The collection activities described in the previous chapter lead to funds in depository and lockbox accounts. These funds must then be transferred into a central account—the *concentration account*—to fund the outflows that normally arise in business: paying vendors, issuing payroll, reducing loans, and/or investing in interest-bearing securities. Concentration and disbursement systems are both tools designed to minimize idle balances and keep cash constantly at work.

Concentration Systems

Companies with large numbers of geographically dispersed stores, such as retail and fast-food chains, require local depositories to receive checks, currency, and credit card receipts (unless transmitted through an in-store modem). As a result, funds often accumulate in collection accounts in various locations. In order to use the funds most effectively, the cash manager needs to concentrate the balances.

Mobilizing Funds

There are a number of options a company can use to move funds into the concentration account.

- *Deposit reporting services.* A deposit reporting service (DRS) functions to assist in the mobilization of funds in local accounts to the concentration account. The store manager contacts the DRS through a toll-free telephone number or a point-of-sale (POS) terminal, and following a series of prompts, reports the store number, the time and amount of the deposit, and any detail required by the company (such as the coin and currency subtotal). The DRS accumulates all of the calls for the company, creates an ACH file to draw down the deposited funds, and transmits the ACH through the banking system. The all-in daily cost per store is approximately $1. There are several DRS vendors, including NDC, First Data, and ADP.

The effectiveness of a DRS system relies on the store manager reporting accurate and timely information. The company can be notified if any store does not contact the DRS, allowing a rapid follow-up to determine the reason for the failure. However, errors will occur if the manager reports a deposit that is not made; a deposit is made after the local bank's cut-off time for ledger credit; or if the amount reported varies from the actual deposit. The result can be overdrafts at the local bank from which the deposits have been concentrated, which can cost $25 in fees for each occurrence.

- *Company-initiated concentration.* Large companies with widespread local offices or stores may develop their own concentration reporting systems. The technology used often involves mini-computer processing, with automated notification by the local site to a treasury function using specified protocols. For example, the stock brokerage industry uses proprietary systems to report each day's activity at branches, details of which include:

  - Checks and securities received by client account

  - Local, national account, and cashier's checks written to pay out funds

  - The amount and time of the deposit

  - Other transactions

  Some of these systems require the branch to input the transit routing numbers of client checks (see Chapter 3) to determine when good funds will be received at the local depository for inclusion in the concentration amount. Treasury prepares the concentration wire transfer or ACHs, based on a cost-benefit calculation for each method.

- *Standing instructions.* The administrative effort necessary to concentrate funds can be alleviated by the issuance of standing instructions to the depository or concentration banks to effect transfers based on various criteria. The criteria could be based on:

- *Frequency.* For example, daily or whenever a "trigger" occurs, usually defined as a collected funds threshold

- *Amount.* For example, any collected funds or only funds exceeding a predetermined target

- *Mechanism.* For example, ACHs for small amounts and Fedwire for large sums as determined by the company's analysis

  Smaller depository banks may not be able to handle such guidelines. In those situations, the concentration bank can initiate a reverse (or drawdown) ACH or Fedwire based on instructions from the DRS or the company.

- *Zero balance accounts (ZBA).* The ZBA structure is used to minimize idle balances in a DDA account. It is an automated service that is used for both the concentration of balances and the funding of disbursement accounts. A master concentration account withdraws any residual balances in individual collection accounts within the same bank network, based on the account holder's standing instructions. The funds can then be used for investment or disbursement purposes.

Concentration System Considerations

Design of a cash concentration system involves considerations of cost and access to information. There are three cost elements to examine in planning a concentration system:

1. *The cost of the transfer mechanism.* Electronic funds transfer systems were discussed in Chapter 2. As noted, there is a significant cost difference between Fedwires and ACH transfers. A Fedwire costs approximately $10 to 15 for a wire out/wire in from the collection account to the concentration account. An ACH transfer is usually about 15 cents for this same journey. However, it should also be noted that costs vary fairly widely for these activities, depending on the extent of automation in ordering the transfer and pricing by individual banks.

2. *The value of the funds in the bank.* Cash sitting in collection and concentration accounts incur an opportunity cost, in that there may be more productive uses for the funds. Some companies establish *tiered concentration systems,* which use multiple levels of concentration accounts to support different corporate businesses. However, any cash in these accounts is earning only a nominal earnings credit rate (ECR—discussed in Chapter 8), which may be several percentage points less than the company's cost of capital.

3. *The opportunity cost of local accounts.* Depository accounts are often used to support the cash requirements of a branch office or other activity distant from corporate headquarters. It may be necessary to leave balances (sometimes called *target balances*) in the accounts for such uses as paying local invoices, emergency disbursements, check encashment, compensation to the bank for its services, or other needs. There is an opportunity cost for these balances, which may be substantial if a company has dozens of local accounts.

The amount of the funds in the collection account should be evaluated to determine if it is cost-effective to use Fedwire (a same-day mechanism) or next-day ACH in order to invest, cover disbursements, or reduce loan balances. For example, $250,000 in a collection account may reduce a loan balance carrying a cost of 10 percent. The value of this amount in repaying the loan for one business day is $100 ($250,000 ÷ 250 business days × 10 percent). If left on deposit in the collection account at an assumed ECR of 2.5 percent, that amount would earn $25 ($250,000 ÷ 250 business days × 2.5 percent). Assuming a Fedwire charge of $15, the company would earn an incremental $60 ($100 - $25 - $15) by making a wire transfer of the collection balance.

Access to information relates to the knowledge that treasury staff has of daily collection balances in depository accounts. Large, decentralized businesses with many local accounts often will not have accurate data on daily receipts and deposits. Smaller companies with fewer sites can more easily exchange information about sales activities and local disbursements

Bank Consolidation

There is no longer any compelling reason for most companies to use extensive networks of banks for cash management. The trend toward bank consolidation (discussed in Chapters 8 and 10) permits fairly broad national coverage through one or two financial institutions. Interstate branching will eliminate or reduce the need to concentrate funds to the extent that collections can be channeled through a single bank.

through e-mail or telephone. The cash manager must weigh the complexity and cost of the system, the burden placed on the local office manager responsible for the deposit and for notifying home office, and the value of the funds transfers in developing the optimal design.

Disbursement Systems

A disbursement system pays vendors, employees, tax agencies, bond- and stockholders, and other payees at the proper time using the appropriate mechanism. As with paper collections, a disbursement system must be managed to reduce idle balances while providing timely disbursement information. Disbursement float arises from the time a check is issued until funds are debited to the payor's account (see Exhibit 4.1).

Mail and clearing float were major considerations in the past when designing a disbursement system, and companies often used remote country points to extend disbursement float. Most companies today are reluctant to send checks from locations distant from their office sites out of concern for the appearance of improper behavior.

Businesses have a number of options in establishing disbursement facilities, as discussed in the following sections.

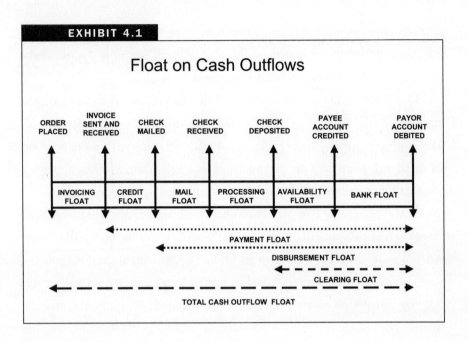

EXHIBIT 4.1

Float on Cash Outflows

Regular Checking

A regular checking account may be established at any commercial bank, and is similar to personal checking used by households. These accounts receive activity during the bank's normal business hours, which effectively means that any holder of a check can request funds from the account (or "cash" the check) at any time. It is also known as an *over-the-counter presentment*. The owner of the account must arrange to either leave balances or transfer funds into the account to cover such activity, or risk the expenses and embarrassment associated with having a check returned for nonsufficient funds (NSF). A good forecasting system can help reduce the level of balances maintained in disbursement accounts (see Chapter 5).

Zero Balance Accounts

As noted in regard to concentration, a ZBA used for disbursements seeks to minimize idle balances in a DDA account. A master account funds the disbursement accounts that have experienced clearings during the day. The net effect is that, at the end of each business day, the balance in each individual account is restored to zero.

The ZBA reduces the number of funding transactions and minimizes funds held in the account(s) awaiting the check clearing process. The issuing company then funds the master account with a Fedwire or an intrabank transfer. This arrangement is often used when companies need to segregate disbursement accounts for accounting reasons.

However, the ZBA approach has one significant disadvantage: Check clearing information is usually not available until the next morning, after the bank has run its DDA system overnight. This procedure results in underutilized funds retained in a bank account to cover clearing checks, or in an overdraft if the required balances are miscalculated.

Controlled Disbursement

In 1983, the Fed established payor bank services, which provides participating banks with information on presentments to be made that day, very early in the morning. This permitted banks to develop controlled disbursement accounts, a specialized form of ZBA account used only for disbursements. The controlled disbursement account is funded once, in the morning, to cover the daily check presentments, eliminating the need for companies to leave balances to cover clearing items. Early notification of checks clearing that day allows funding of the account on a same-day basis and helps the cash manager determine the company's cash position.

These accounts are established in regional check processing centers (RCPCs) or country points to which the Federal Reserve delivers the clearing checks (or cash letter or a data file of clearing items) in the early morning. Banks with more than $10 million in average daily clearings from banks outside their Fed district receive a second presentment from the Fed through the High Dollar Group Sort (HDGS). As the result, these banks provide two clearing notifications to issuing companies:

1. The first presentment amount, available by about 8:30 A.M., normally covers some 75 percent of the total day's debit.

2. The second presentment amount, available by 10:00 A.M., contains all of that day's clearing dollars.

The impact of disbursing through a bank with a second presentment is that the cash position is not known until later in the day and is, therefore, of little help to the cash manager in determining the daily cash position. HDGS is intended to discourage disbursing from a geographically remote location. Exhibit 4.2 has a current list of banks and their controlled disbursement locations.

EXHIBIT 4.2

Controlled Disbursement Sites

Bank	Locations	
ABN AMRO—LaSalle Bank N.A.	Chicago RCPC	
Allfirst Bank	Millsboro DE	
AmSouth Bank	Jasper AL	
Bank of America	Asheville NC	Vandalia MO
	DeKalb GA	Walnut Creek CA
	Northbrook IL	Wichita Falls TX
	Tallahassee FL	
Bank of New York	White Plains NY	Wilmington DE
Bank of Oklahoma	Henryetta OK	Wewoka OK
Bank One	Circleville OH	Port Arthur TX
	Dearborn MI	Wilmington DE
	Evanston IN	
Citibank	Wilmington DE	
Comerica Bank	Ann Arbor MI	

EXHIBIT 4.2 CONTINUED

Controlled Disbursement Sites

Bank	Locations	
Deutsche Bank	Wilmington DE	
First Interstate	Billings MT	
Fleet	Hartford CT	Portland ME
Harris Bank	Roselle IL	
JPMorgan Chase	San Angelo TX	Wilmington DE
	Syracuse NY	
KeyBank	Albany NY	Price UT
	Anchorage AK	Vermilion OH
	Portland ME	
M & T	Ithaca NY	Wilkes-Barre PA
	Newburgh NY	
Mellon Bank	Everett MA	Wilmington DE
	Pittsburgh RCPC	
National City Bank	Ashland OH	
Northern Trust	DuPage IL	
PNC Bank	Jeannette PA	
Sovereign Bank	Braintree MA	
SunTrust Banks	Rome GA	Sevierville TN
U.S. Bancorp	Aspen CO	Memphis MO
	East Grand Forks MN	Miamisburg OH
	Havre MT	Wausau WI
Union Planters Bank	Goreville IL	New Holland IL
Wachovia Bank	Augusta GA	Wilmington DE
	Chapel Hill NC	Winston-Salem NC
	Greenville SC	
Wells Fargo Bank	Calabasas CA	Plano TX
	Grand Junction CO	Redwing MT
	Lewistown MT	Van Wert OH

Source: Phoenix-Hecht 2003 Cash Management Monitor

Remote Disbursing to Gain Float

Banks establish their controlled disbursement sites at locations that are difficult to reach and are only served by the Federal Reserve check clearing system. Consequently, float can be extended (by one-fourth to one-third of a business day, according to Phoenix-Hecht studies) by using these relatively inaccessible sites. Although the lengthening of clearing float through a controlled disbursement account is feasible, the finance profession and the Federal Reserve have long-established policies against the appearance of disbursing "remotely" to gain float.

Unless a company is located in a rural location in such states as Montana, Utah, and Colorado, the intention of extending float will be fairly obvious to check recipients. The ill will that may result is probably not worth the slight float gain, and it is generally not recommended. A better alternative is simply to diary payments for one additional day but use a bank located in the company's state of domicile.

The relative inaccessibility of these locations minimizes the possibility of an over-the-counter presentment during the day. Most banks offering controlled disbursement will hold any checks so received, or will make clearing adjustments the next day for debit to the account, eliminating supplemental funds transfers to cover any shortfall.

Several features of controlled disbursement provide advantages for the check issuance and funding process. In addition, various control and reconciliation products support controlled disbursement to minimize potential occurrences of fraud or accounting mistakes. Each of these will be discussed in the sections that follow.

Funding

A major advantage of controlled disbursement is a morning notification by the bank of the clearing total from the Federal Reserve's cash letter presentment. The bank notifies the company electronically at about 10:00 A.M. (local time), based on the information transmitted through payor bank services, without waiting for the delivery of checks—the cash letter—to arrive. This information is available to the company through various mechanisms, including telephone, fax, and the bank's computerized information reporting system. The company then has until a specified time later in the day (usually the close of business) to fund the resulting debit.

Funding options include intrabank transfer, a wire transfer from the company's concentration bank, or an ACH credit. The ACH credit does not become "good" funds until the next business day, so the controlled disbursement bank will require the equivalent of the average check clearings of one or more days to be maintained in the account to cover the ACH float.

Positive Pay

Positive pay is the most important control and fraud prevention concept available for checks. After each day's check run, the company sends a file to its bank, which contains data on all issued items. The issued file is delivered by magnetic tape or through a PC modem transmission. The bank merges the daily file with data on all previously issued checks that have not yet been presented for clearing. When the cash letter arrives at the bank the following morning, clearing items are matched against issued items.

Positive Pay and Fraud Prevention

Mismatches of clearing and issued items by check number and dollar amount are reported to the company through the bank's computerized reporting system. The company has a period of time (usually about four or five hours) to decide whether to authorize or reject the payment of each item. Manual reconciliation, discussed in the next section, can detect a fraud, but on a seriously time-delayed basis. Positive pay attacks the problem each day as checks clear against the bank, offering a first line of defense against a fraudulent check.

With the FBI estimating the extent of fraud at $5 to $10 billion a year in the United States, banks have begun to insist that businesses using their disbursement products accept positive pay. This is accomplished in two ways:

1. Consistent with UCC Article 4A provisions (discussed in Chapter 8), some banks will not accept any liability for fraudulent checks unless positive pay service is used.

2. Other banks are now pricing disbursement services to include positive pay with controlled disbursement rather than as a separate service.

The most common reasons legitimate checks are not included in the issued file are emergencies that occur after the regular check run or as disbursements from branch locations. In those situations, the data from those checks should be entered into the next daily positive pay file transmission. Should that not occur, a "mismatch" will result. The other cause of a mismatch is an attempted fraud, such as when a legitimate check is altered for a larger sum or when a completely counterfeit check is created using invalid check numbers and dollar amounts.

When the company receives notification of any mismatches, it should research each item to determine whether the cause was innocent or an attempt at fraud. This requires determining who authorized the check, what the purpose of the payment was, and whether a crime may be occurring. The bank will need a decision before the Fed deadlines so that it can return any rejected checks through the banking system. To protect itself, the bank will require a default decision of "pay" or "don't pay" at the time that the service is established.

Positive Pay Is Not Perfect

Positive pay may not be able to prevent a fraudulent check from being cashed at a bank teller line since only a few banks currently have teller online access to the issue file. The best interim protection is to work with the banks to develop a program that assures positive identification for check cashing, such as a company-issued photo identification and two other proofs of identity. Furthermore, positive pay cannot catch a counterfeit endorsement or prevent encashment of a fraudulent item in good faith by a check cashing exchange.

Other Disbursement Services

Services that support controlled disbursing include reconciliation, stop payments, and safekeeping.

Reconciliation

Monthly reconciliation is necessary to determine that the bank's records and company ledgers are in agreement, and that neither party has made an error that goes uncorrected. In fact, UCC Article 4 (see Chapter 8) requires that companies examine bank statements within a reasonable time frame, not to exceed 30 days after the statement has been sent, and to report to the bank any unauthorized signatures or alterations.

Companies typically receive bank statements about 15 days after the end of the month, including cancelled checks and advices of other debits or credits. Reconciliation clerks add any deposits made after the statement closing date to the bank's ending balance, subtract the total of any checks still outstanding, and make any necessary correcting entries to balance the bank and company ledgers. This process should reveal any fraud, but a month or more might pass before an investigation begins.

Banks can now provide automated partial or full reconciliation to the company within 5 to 10 days of month-end. Partial reconciliation (or "recon") is simply a list of paid or cleared items, including check number and dollar amount that the company must then reconcile against its own ledgers. Full recon involves a matching of issued and clearing items by the bank, with reports on items:

- Issued and paid (or cleared)
- Issued but not yet paid
- Paid but not issued: that is, not entered on the daily issued file
- Force posted: items that involve duplicate check numbers due to check printing errors or fraud

Full recon is typically provided in a positive pay environment because the bank already has the issued file and needs no further input.

IN THE REAL WORLD

Manual Reconciliation and Fraud Detection

Manual reconciliation has generally been an imperfect mechanism to detect fraud. In one situation, a company issued a legitimate payment for $80. The check was altered to $8,000, by adding two zeros, and presented for payment. Four months passed before the recon clerks discovered the fraud. Investigators could find no trace of the criminal responsible and the company had to accept the $7,720 loss.

Stop Payments

A company may determine that a check was issued in error or as a duplicate payment. The check can be "stopped," or prevented from being honored by the bank, through the issuance of instructions directing that the item be rejected if presented for clearing. Stops can be initiated through the bank's electronic banking platform, by telephone, or fax. Stop payments typically are valid for six months and must be renewed thereafter.

Check Safekeeping

Banks will store cancelled checks on their premises for 60 to 90 days, and then create copies of each check (front and back) in microfilm, microfiche, or imaging technology. The copy can be provided to the company for research in the form of film, fiche, or CD-ROM. Alternatively, the bank will store and reproduce the check copy for a fee if so directed. Courts now accept check copies as proof of a payment or in fraud investigations, allowing the destruction of the paper item.

Check Fraud Prevention

While positive pay has significantly reduced the incidence of check fraud, disbursement systems have numerous other potential areas for criminal attack. Other actions to reduce fraud include the following (in sequence order):

Prior to issuance:

1. Secure check stock and signature plates, and allow only authorized staff to have access to the treasury locations where they are stored. Maintain logs of use, including check number runs.

2. Verify vendors used in the purchasing-accounts payable cycle. Fraud may occur in purchasing through the use of fictitious vendors. Vendors should be reviewed for legitimacy by the following actions:

- Require a federal tax identification number
- Conduct a credit check on the vendor using a credit agency
- Obtain an audited financial statement
- Visit the vendor's premises
- Request references from other customers

Issuance:

1. Print checks on blank safety paper using laser check-printing equipment. Rather than signing checks by signature plate, print the signature or a substitute at the time the check is printed. Substitutes for signatures include unique characters, Greek letters, or other typographical marks.

2. Consolidate check issuance and close local accounts opened for the convenience of branch expenses. All checks should be issued from a central site under the supervision of designated employees.

Post-issuance:

1. Keep all checks in a secure area within treasury. Do not allow company employees to pick up checks for individual transmittal, and do not allow vendors to stop by for hand delivery of payments.

2. Review all positive pay mismatches to ascertain that approved items are legitimate payments and not attempts at fraud.

Policies and procedures:

1. Work with local banks to prevent check fraud. Insist that checks presented for payment are supported by multiple identifications, including a driver's license, a credit card, and, if the check is for payroll, an employee photo ID.

2. Limit authorized signers to a few senior corporate officers. A company with numerous branch locations can have hundreds of authorized check signers. Although banks do not verify signatures except when checks are deposited through a teller, controls on approved signers can improve the possibility of preventing or proving a fraud.

3. Separate the function of maintaining the approved vendor file from other activities, and do not allow vendors to be added by purchasing clerks.

Electronic Check Presentment

Certain banking institutions use electronic check presentment (ECP) to reduce the risk of fraud. The depository bank captures the MICR-line from the check and transmits it electronically to the drawee bank. The drawee bank can then review the checks-issued file and determine if any item is a mismatch one or two days before the paper check clears. (The actual check clearing process is based on the paper check, not the ECP). Checks transmitted through ECP constitute less than 5 percent of all check volume, with the Fed handling about three-quarters of all ECP volume. (The governing organization is the Electronic Check Clearing House Organization (ECCHO), whose Web site is located at *www.eccho.com*.)

A related program is *check truncation,* where the paper item is not returned to the issuing company and all funding and reconciliation is from the MICR-line data. Typically, a copy of the check is captured through imaging, which is then provided through a CD-ROM, paper, or an Internet download.

Payroll

The payment of wages and salary has gradually migrated to direct deposit by ACH electronic transfers, although many payrolls support both direct deposit and checks. The usage of electronic transfers is probably one-half of all payroll transactions, but exceeds 80 percent in California and certain other locations.

Direct Deposit Mechanics

The employee provides a voided check from his or her bank account to the payroll department. TRN data (see Chapter 3) from the bottom of the check is used to build a file record of the bank address, the account number, and the net amount to be paid. Depending on the arrangement with the disbursement bank, the ACH transfer is made one or two days before the pay date. This assures that good funds will be in the employee's account on pay date.

The primary advantages of this process are:

- Lower cost to the employer, in that the cost of an ACH is about 10 percent or less of the all-in cost of a check.

- Reduced employee absence, as there is no reason for the employee to leave company premises to deposit or cash the payroll check.

- Convenience for the employee, as the pay is in the bank regardless of weather, vacation, business travel, or the loss of the payroll envelope.

- Fraud prevention, as there is no need to verify the identification of an employee attempting to cash a payroll check.

Disadvantages include the following:

- The employer loses all use of the funds deposited for the payroll—the float—on pay date. Studies of payroll check clearing show that the average delay in check clearing is about three business days. The value of this float loss could be considerable; for example, a $500,000 weekly payroll would cost about $30,000 a year in lost float if entirely converted to direct deposit ($500,000 × 10% ÷ 5 days × 3 days).

- The funds are credited to the employee's account, the earnings on which, depending on the type of account, may or may not accrue to his or her benefit.

- The employer must manage a dual payroll system—check and direct deposit—unless all pays are converted to electronic. This is not a major concern for most companies because a payroll services vendor is often used for payrolls. Leading companies include ADP, Interpay, and Paychex.

Paycards

For employees not wishing to receive a check (because of problems of encashment or security), several banks offer payroll ATM cards. The employee need not have an account at the payroll bank; instead, an ATM card is issued along with a PIN number, allowing access through any ATM machine or at merchants that accept the card "family" (e.g., Visa or MasterCard). The employee receives a monthly statement detailing withdrawals, payroll credits, and purchases.

IN THE REAL WORLD

Resistance to Direct Deposit

Employees who resist direct deposit typically do so for one of the following reasons: they want to hide pay from a spouse or significant other, do not have a bank account, or are simply uninformed about the mechanics of the program. Companies can require direct deposit as a condition of employment, but must allow employees to select the financial institution to which their pay is sent.

Educational programs conducted by human resources or a local bank may help to overcome resistance. Many companies find that a bank is only too happy to market its services to a new audience through a year's free checking, discounted mortgage or home loans, free credit card programs, or other promotions.

If there is sufficient employment at a single site, the bank may be willing to install an ATM for employee banking (which the company may have to subsidize). A collateral advantage is eliminating petty cash maintained to accommodate check cashing and travel or expense reimbursement. In addition to the management and replenishment of these funds, the company avoids the risk of theft.

Purchasing-Accounts Payable Cycle

The purchasing-accounts payable cycle involves extensive paperwork, including requisitions, purchase orders, receiving reports, and payment approvals. This process has been estimated to cost in excess of $100 per transaction. To avoid this cost (except for sophisticated and technical purchases), several banks and credit card issuers now offer procurement cards.

Procurement Cards

Procurement cards (also known as *purchasing cards*) are essentially like corporate credit or debit cards that are issued to designated employees to make purchases on behalf of the company. However, they differ in the following respects:

- The company receives the bill and is responsible for payment.
- Codes are embedded in the card to restrict purchases to eligible types of products and services, and to limit the total amount spent.
- Automated data capture enables the company to receive next-day summaries of purchasing activities.

Purchasing can be simplified through the use of the cards for routine items. A major procurement card benefit is the elimination of the paperwork inherent in creating a purchase order (sometimes called a PO). In addition, volume discounts may be arranged with vendors frequently used, and employees can be encouraged or instructed to use those suppliers.

Savings arising from procurement card programs can be 80 to 90 percent of the cost of the traditional purchase order cycle. In establishing the program, companies frequently develop efficiencies through the reengineering of elements of the purchasing/accounts payable cycle. Opposition has been primarily from purchasing departments, which see these cards as a threat to their position in the company. However, widespread card usage has minimized this problem, particularly as management is generally pleased with the savings typically achieved.

Other Potential Improvements

The purchasing-accounts payable disbursement cycle offers various other opportunities for efficiencies:

- *Cash discounts.* The lengthy payables cycle for items acquired through purchase orders requires a match against receiving reports (sometimes called *receivers*) prior to the approval for payment. A review of this process may reveal missed cash discount opportunities when vendor invoices are not paid within the discount period, often 10 days from the receipt of the invoice (as in "2/10, net 30").

- *Early release of payments.* Some invoices are paid early, before the stated date on the invoice or the date established by company policy. This often results from a "clean desk" policy, where companies require paperwork to be "cleared" from work areas as soon as all documentation is compiled, regardless of time value of money considerations (see Chapter 1).

TIPS & TECHNIQUES

Overcoming Opposition from Purchasing Departments

Some companies have overcome opposition to procurement card programs by emphasizing the advantage of the elimination of routine buying from purchasing department processing. With middle managers deciding on basic purchases, purchasing professionals can spend their time on procurement decisions that require technological, systems, and engineering expertise.

Payments should not be released prior to the date established by vendor terms (e.g., net 30 days) or by company policy (e.g., no payment will be issued before 35 days have passed since the invoice was received).

- *Missing documentation.* Frequently, vendor invoices are not completely reviewed, in contradiction to basic control procedures. Accounting codes and authorized signatures may not be verified, and the necessary documentation in support of the payment is often missing.

  - Accounting codes are used both to debit budgets for expenditures and to assure that spending has not exceeded approved limits.

  - Authorized signatures are necessary to assure that the requested payment has been reviewed at the appropriate management level. Payables departments cannot be expected to validate hundreds of signatures, some of which are illegible. It is good practice to periodically purge the list of accepted signers.

IN THE REAL WORLD

Early Payments

Early payments—that is, before the established due date—are often made to important vendors who seek preferential treatment by the payables staff. In some cases, the amounts involved constitute some of the largest purchases regularly remitted by a company. Computer salespeople have been known to pick up checks in person, rather than wait for the check printing–mailing cycle. In one situation, an analysis of the accounts payable function found that the average early payment was made on day 22, 8 days before the date stated on the invoice (day 30). This resulted in an annual opportunity cost of about $60,000.

- Supporting documentation should include POs, receivers, and vendor contracts; any payment request missing such reports should be rejected.

Comprehensive Payables

Several banks offer a complete disbursement outsourcing service often referred to as *comprehensive payables*. The company prepares a file in any of several formats containing the following payment data:

- Due date of payment (as payments can be warehoused by the bank)
- Dollar amount
- Payee and payee's address
- Mechanism (e.g., check, Fedwire, ACH or EDI)
- Accompanying remittance detail

The bank creates payments as instructed and issues them on a date specified by the company. Some banks determine the appropriate pay-

---

TIPS & TECHNIQUES

Authority to Approve Expenditures

Managers should not be given blanket authority to approve any type of company expense. The following language in policy and procedures manuals has actually been used: ". . . company officers with the rank of vice president or above may approve a check request in any amount." This mandate could result in inappropriate (and potentially embarrassing or even fraudulent) expenditures not related to the business purpose of the organization. However, the accounts payable function would be powerless to intervene.

ment mechanism based on company-determined parameters. Electronic payments are issued as requested by the company and are charged based on the bank's standard pricing.

Payments by Check

Checks are prepared for mailing, including any remittance detail required by the issuer. Information typically provides invoice or item number(s) being paid and adjustments to the invoiced amount, including discounts taken or credits for damaged merchandise. Certain industries require lengthy descriptions of payments, such as *explanation of benefits* (EOB) statements provided to insureds and healthcare providers by insurance companies.

Most comprehensive payables banks can process all of this material, including the envelope. The bank can also print company logos, signature lines, and promotional statements, such as "ask us about e-commerce." Inexpensive desktop technology allows the issuance of emergency checks and the transmission of a supplemental-issued file to the bank.

The payment is prepared for delivery; postage is applied and mailed. The bank will attempt to gain the highest postal discount offered by the USPS for quantity mailings, currently 4.5 cents (as of mid-year 2002). As the checks clear, the bank performs the usual positive pay service and funds the resulting daily debit based on instructions from the company. In addition, reconciliation and check storage are provided.

Benefits

There are significant benefits to companies using the comprehensive payables service.

- *Consolidation of the payments function.* Instead of having to maintain different systems for the different payment types, companies can now use a single file and system for all disbursements.

- *Outsourcing the entire check printing/mailing/reconciliation process.* Several internal company responsibilities can be entirely eliminated, and the risk of internal fraud is significantly diminished by handing over the process to a bank.

- *Cost savings.* Studies indicate that the all-in cost of creating and sending a payment is approximately $5, although fees vary by issuing organization. Banks are currently bidding the service for about 50 cents, plus postage, for paper disbursements. Electronic disbursements are charged at the bank's price for ACH, EDI, or Fedwire, with an additional charge for managing the disbursement process. The company continues to have some expenses for general bank contact, including overall supervision and the daily "pay" or "no pay" positive pay decision. A rough estimate of the cost of using a bank for outsourced payments is $1 per transaction.

Summary

Concentration systems are designed to mobilize cash in bank accounts for the benefit of the business: to fund disbursements, repay loans, or invest. However, funds mobilization is undergoing significant changes with the Interstate Banking and Branching Efficiency Act (see Chapter 8), making it possible to concentrate funds in one step by collecting through the branches of a single bank network.

Appropriate disbursement mechanisms must be selected for the entire disbursement cycle—purchasing, accounts payable, and payment issuance—in the context of cost, convenience, control over possible fraud, and access to bank systems. The outsourcing of portions of the disbursement process has become a viable and economic alternative to the traditional check-writing function. The transformation of disbursement systems from paper to electronic is occurring, although somewhat slowly, with the most notable use being the direct deposit of payroll.

After hearing a presentation from their bankers, Ann and Bill realized the extent of their exposure to fraud by not using positive pay. They also became aware of the inherent inefficiencies of their decentralized disbursement system. Of the 5,000 disbursement checks issued each year, about half were to vendors, with the other half for payroll. While some direct deposit was used, efforts to encourage greater acceptance had been nominal. As the result of their analysis, Ann and Bill resolved to:

- Consolidate concentration banks to a single bank network. *This action would remove idle balances in collection accounts, reduce the volume of funds transfers, eliminate some bank fees, and strengthen credit and cash management links to one financial institution.*

- Actively promote direct deposit (in cooperation with the payroll department). *This would reduce the number of checks issued, the check reconciliation burden, and the risk of the theft or loss of a pay check, while providing a convenience to their employees. One of their banks agreed to provide six months of free checking for any employee who signed up for the service.*

- Implement positive pay and full reconciliation. *Besides pleasing their auditors with the heightened control and fraud prevention, positive pay would actually reduce the per-check charge from 15 cents to 9 cents. Full recon would eliminate the need for three accounting clerks, whose job was to perform the monthly reconciliations.*

- Centralize disbursements. *Decentralized check writing requires the maintenance of checkbooks at 12 locations, significant costs in maintaining balances in local bank accounts, and delayed notification to treasury of checks written. Centralizing this function would reduce costs, improve controls, and increase the timeliness of accounting.*

91

Although intrigued with the comprehensive payables product, Bill realized that centralization of the disbursement function was a necessary first step before comprehensive payables could be considered.

CHAPTER 5

Liquidity Management

After reading this chapter, you will be able to

- Understand the tools of liquidity management

- Review the major forecasting techniques used by cash managers

- Examine the issues that are important in short-term borrowing and investing

- Identify the elements that influence investment and borrowing rates

- Learn how to compare different instruments and their effective yields or costs

CASE STUDY

Seasonal cash flows are a problem facing many of GETDOE's divisions. Over 70 percent of sales occur during a three-month period. Treasurer Bill Fold is hopeful that reorganization of the cash management department into a centralized unit will uncover excess cash that can be used to even out the liquidity problems of these cyclical businesses. Bill understands that a good forecasting system is essential to managing liquidity effectively, so he asks his cash manager, Ann I. Shade, to review the current system and make recommendations.

> Ann's challenge is to institute a new companywide cash management forecasting system that will:
>
> - Accurately predict expected cash inflows and outflows for all business units
>
> - Be flexible enough to reflect changes in the market or competitive environment
>
> - Provide early identification of expected deficits or surpluses so that reasonable credit terms can be negotiated
>
> Ann is also refining the company's liquidity management guidelines for the new centralized organization. She has suggested that Bill prepare formal policies on short-term investment and borrowing. The document will specify GETDOE's financing objectives, acceptable instruments, maturities, appetite for risk, diversification, and acceptable counterparties.

Liquidity Management

Liquidity refers to a company's cash position and its ability to meet obligations when due. A key role of all cash managers in ensuring liquidity is the daily monitoring of working capital to optimally manage the company's resources by accelerating inflows and controlling outflows. If there is an excess of cash in the daily position, the cash manager has to determine the best use for that surplus. If there is a deficit, the cash manager must find a source of funds. Exhibit 5.1 illustrates the liquidity management cycle.

Cash managers control liquidity by ensuring that they have a sufficient reserve of liquid assets or access to borrowing facilities to cover the company's immediate cash requirements. A *liquid asset* is one that can be easily and rapidly converted into cash without loss of value. The goal is to provide a safety net in the event of a shortfall in cash, as well

EXHIBIT 5.1

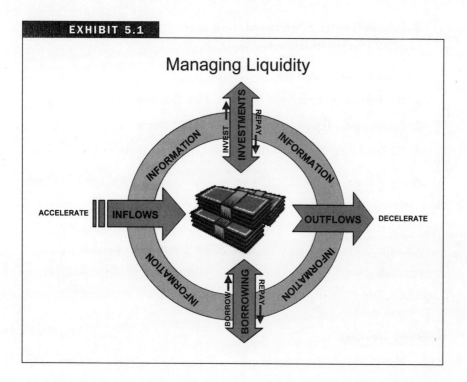

Managing Liquidity

as to establish a resource for future acquisitions or capital expenditures.

Solvency and liquidity are different concepts. *Solvency* is an accounting term that refers to the net position of a company's assets minus liabilities. It is possible for a solvent company (i.e., one that has more assets than liabilities on its books) to go bankrupt. It is equally possible for an insolvent company, when protected by the bankruptcy laws that freeze liabilities, to build up liquidity through ongoing operations and the sale of assets.

Sources and Uses of Liquidity

There are three major sources and uses of liquidity. The sources are:

1. *Business flows.* Cash generated by the business

2. *Internal sources.* Cash on deposit or invested in liquid instruments

3. *External sources.* Cash raised from sources such as the commercial paper market or from banks

The three major uses are:

1. *Business flows.* Outflows generated by the business

2. *Internal uses.* Investments or purchase of assets

3. *External uses.* Repayment of debt or investments

A company must have sufficient reserves not only for expected outflows but also for unanticipated shortfalls; for example, a customer payment not being received when expected or a check being returned for insufficient funds. There are also occasions when a business opportunity arises unexpectedly, such as an offer of excess inventory at distressed prices. Liquidity allows a company to take advantage of such opportunities.

Managing Liquidity

The cash manager's task is to determine exactly the right amount of liquidity to maintain, given the company's business, operations, and cash flow patterns. Too much liquidity results in cash being used inefficiently, which may result in a loss of earnings, also known as *opportunity cost.* Too little liquidity can have consequences ranging from small to considerable, such as:

- Extra fees or interest costs for late payments
- Using more expensive funds transfer methods
- Higher cost of borrowing
- Missed trade discounts
- Lost business opportunities
- Legal fees
- Tarnished business reputation
- Customer and supplier defections
- Bankruptcy and liquidation

Accuracy in cash forecasting will directly impact the cash manager's ability to invest and borrow short-term funds on favorable terms. The best time to invest or borrow funds is early in the morning, when the money markets are active and liquid. Toward the end of the day, investment and borrowing opportunities become fewer, and rates are less attractive. Cash managers who can predict a shortfall well in advance are more likely to be able to put alternative sources of funding in place at a reasonable cost. One of the most expensive forms of credit is last-minute, unanticipated borrowing. Controlled disbursement products (discussed in Chapter 4) are specifically designed to provide cash managers with disbursement information early in the day so that any surpluses or shortfalls can be covered or invested when markets are still active.

Cash Forecasting

Cash forecasting is used to estimate the liquidity position of the company for periods ranging from the current day up to one year. Short-term forecasts (0–3 months) are used primarily for managing liquidity. Operational forecasts (1–12 months) are used for medium term working capital and financing requirements. Long-term forecasts (1–5 years) are used for planning strategic financial goals. Forecasting methods used by cash managers are discussed in the sections that follow.

Cash Budgeting

The simple cash budget, or forecast, combines what is known about expected receipts (e.g., collections from customers, interest, and maturing investments) with expected disbursements (e.g., expected check presentments, payroll, taxes, interest payments, and loan repayments). The result is then adjusted for other factors, including the certainty and reliability of these estimates.

This forecast is done on a daily, weekly, or monthly basis, and is used to estimate anticipated cash shortfalls or excesses. Many of the bank services described in Chapters 3 and 4 are designed to assist the cash manager in forecasting receipts and disbursements. Exhibit 5.2 illustrates a cash budget. The funding of deficits and investment of surpluses are assumed to be settled by the end of each month.

The Distribution Method

With sufficient historical data on cash flows, the cash manager can prepare a distribution forecast based on past patterns of activity. Some distribution forecasts combine several factors, such as days since distribution with day-of-the-week, when there is an interrelated and predictable pattern of cash activity. Exhibit 5.3 illustrates a schedule that would be used to predict the clearing of payroll checks. The combined percentages would be applied to the total disbursement to allow the cash manager to anticipate daily cash outflows.

EXHIBIT 5.2

Cash Budget

	APRIL	MAY	JUNE
Cash Receipts	$25,000	$18,000	$22,500
Cash Payments	–$17,650	–$27,750	–$18,500
Net Cash Position	$7,350	–$9,750	$4,000
Opening Cash Position	$2,555	$9,905	$155
Ending Cash Position	$9,905	$155	$4,155
Target Balance	–$5,000	–$5,000	–$5,000
Fund Deficit		–$4,845	–$845
Invest Surplus	$4,905		

EXHIBIT 5.3

Distribution Forecast

Business Days after Check Issued	Percent of Value Expected to Clear	Day of Week	Percent Effect
1	35	Monday	−5
2	25	Tuesday	0
3	20	Wednesday	−2
4	10	Thursday	+2
5	10	Friday	+5

Expected distribution of a $250,000 payroll on Wednesday June 7.

Date	Business Day after Issue	Day of Week	Percent Expected to Clear	Clearing Forecast
June 8	1	Thursday	35 + 2 = 37	$92,500
June 9	2	Friday	25 + 5 = 30	$75,000
June 12	3	Monday	20 − 5 = 15	$37,500
June 13	4	Tuesday	10 + 0 = 10	$25,000
June 14	5	Wednesday	10 − 2 = 8	$20,000

Cash Modeling

Cash modeling is used for longer-term forecasts. Again, using historical data, it is possible to extrapolate relationships between certain elements of the profit and loss statement and the balance sheet. For example, the revenue associated with sales will have a direct correlation with the cost of goods sold, levels of inventory, payables, and receivables. Similarly, the amount and contractual interest rate of a company's debt will determine future interest payment obligations.

The cash manager can prepare a projected financial statement based on the company's forecast for elements such as sales, expense levels, debt, and dividends for the following year. Exhibit 5.4 illustrates an analysis based on forecasted levels of activity, including a 15 percent increase in sales and a reduction in long-term debt. The resulting pro forma statement will indicate whether the forecast for the next year will result in a surplus or deficit. In the example, the forecast projects a surplus of $59,000. The treasurer can now make decisions concerning adjustments that need to be made to debt, investments, dividends, inventory levels, and other assets or liabilities for the next year.

Regression Analysis

Regression analysis is a more complex statistical technique, usually performed using a computer. The procedure determines the relationship between the variable being forecast (the dependent variable) and various independent variables. Data concerning the independent elements provides a basis for predicting the value of the variable to be forecast.

EXHIBIT 5.4

Cash Modeling: Pro Forma Financials
($000s)

PROFIT AND LOSS	ACTUAL	PROJECTED		BALANCE SHEET	ACTUAL	PROJECTED
Sales	4000	4600		Cash	350	403
Cost of Goods Sold	−3000	−3450		Receivables	500	575
Selling/Admin Costs	−500	−575		Inventory	200	230
Depreciation	−100	−85		Net Assets	650	565
Interest Expense	−31	−16				
				Total Assets	1700	1773
Income before Tax	369	474				
Tax @40%	−148	−190		Payables	650	748
Net Income	221	284				
				Long-Term Debt	350	200
Dividends		−100		Equity	700	884
Retained Earnings		184				
				Total Liabilities	1700	1832
				Net Surplus		59

Based on projected 15 percent increase in sales and reduction of long-term debt to $200,000

For example, a regression analysis of retail sales activity (the dependent variable) may determine that there is a significant correlation with three factors (the independent variables): the day of the week, prices charged, and advertising within the past week. A regression analysis takes the relevant factors into account to forecast daily sales.

Choosing a Forecasting Method

In considering which forecasting techniques to use, the cash manager has to weigh a number of factors.

- *Availability of data.* Using information that is readily available makes it possible for the cash manager to produce a timely forecast. Unfortunately, businesses typically do not maintain data in formats that allow easy access for statistical analysis.

- *Reliability of data.* In producing the forecast, the cash manager will have to assess the probability of being correct about the timing of cash flows.

  - *Assured cash flows.* For example, tax payments, dividends, debt repayments, and maturing investments. These can be forecast with a very high degree of reliability.

  - *Reliable cash flows.* For example, collections from credit sales, total hourly payroll, and vendor payments. These can be predicted within an acceptable range of accuracy.

  - *Unreliable cash flows.* For example, foreign currency collections, the outcome of pending lawsuits, and costs of work stoppages. The timing and the value of these flows are extremely difficult to forecast.

  - *Unanticipated cash flows.* For example, cash inflows or outflows resulting from totally unexpected circumstances such as the outbreak of war in an area where the company is involved, or the opportunity to buy up inventory due to a competitor going out of business.

101

The nature of the flow and past experience will help the cash manager assign a probability factor to individual elements in the forecast.

- *Time horizon.* The more distant in time the forecast, the less accurate and the less useful it becomes to the cash manager. Five-year forecasts are rarely revisited after the initial effort, and quickly become outdated unless they are continuously revised. Cash managers need to make sure that the time horizon for their forecast is appropriate for the intended purpose.

- *Sensitivity.* Things change, and the cash manager must be prepared to review, refine, and adjust the forecast frequently in light of internal and external amendments.

Instruments for Short-Term Investing

Cash managers frequently have temporary short-term surpluses for investment in appropriate vehicles. These surpluses arise from cash flows from the business, variable sales pattern, the sale of assets or investments, and from raising capital or debt. Market conditions will sometimes dictate when a company raises funds, which may be sooner than the anticipated outflow, resulting in a temporary surplus.

The return, or yield, on an investment is influenced by many factors, but is primarily a reflection of the risk associated with the specific issuer. The market recognizes three broad categories of issuers: government, banks, and companies. The major short-term investment instruments used by cash managers are listed in order of increasing default risk.

Government Instruments

Government securities, considered to have the lowest risk of default, include the following:

- *U.S. Treasury securities* are backed by the full faith and credit of the U.S. government and are deemed by the markets to be risk-free as direct obligations of the Treasury. Treasury Bills (T-Bills) are highly liquid due to their credit quality and short-term maturities, ranging from three months to one year. Treasury Notes have maturities from 1 to 10 years. Treasury Bonds are issued for maturities of greater than 10 years. Treasury Notes and Treasury Bonds are available either as fixed-rate or inflation-indexed investments.

- *Agency securities* are also considered to be very low credit risk investments, although only two of them are backed by the full faith and credit of the U.S. government: the Government National Mortgage Association (Ginnie Maes) and the Department of Veterans Affairs (Vinnie Macs). These instruments are generally very liquid, and many of them are partially exempt from state and local income taxes. Other agency securities include the Federal National Mortgage Association (Fannie Mae) and the Federal Home Loan Mortgage Corporation (Freddie Mac).

- *State and local government municipal obligations.* The risk of the instrument depends on the condition of the issuer, the purpose of the debt, and the time to maturity. Most municipal issues are *revenue securities,* backed by the revenue streams and future earnings that are generated by specific projects, such as tolls from roads or rental income from leased facilities (i.e., a new airport). *General obligation securities,* which are backed by the full faith and credit of the issuer, are repaid from taxes and any other source of income to meet the debt payments. Not all authorities, however, have the power to tax. Municipalities also issue certificates of participation where securities are issued for large capital investments, which in turn are pledged as collateral for the issue. Municipal obligations are generally exempt from federal taxes.

Bank Instruments

Bank instruments typically offer a higher yield than U.S. Treasuries due to the perceived greater bank risk and lower liquidity. A distinction is made between investments with banks located in the United States and banks that are offshore. A deposit placed with a bank in New York City will be considered less risky and will, therefore, pay a lower rate of interest than a deposit placed with that same bank's Cayman Islands or London branch. The following are some of the principal bank-issued investments.

- *Time deposits.* Time deposits are fixed-period, fixed-rate, short-term bank deposits, although banks will often allow early termination with an interest penalty. Eurodollar time deposits are full-liability U.S. dollar-denominated deposits in an offshore branch of a U.S. bank, a foreign bank, or in an International Banking Facility (IBF). A majority of money in the Eurodollar market is held in Eurodollar time deposits.

- *Certificates of deposit (CDs).* CDs are interest-bearing deposits with maturities ranging from seven days to a few years. They are often negotiable and sold on the secondary market. CDs are available in fixed- or floating-rate form. Yankee CDs are U.S. dollar-denominated CDs sold by foreign banks in the United States. Banks outside the United States issue Eurodollar CDs.

- *Bankers' acceptances (BAs).* BAs are short-term bank obligations that arise from a commercial trade transaction. BAs facilitate loans, particularly between importers and investors. They arise when a loan is made by a bank in the form of a short-term negotiable discount time draft drawn on and accepted by the issuing bank. BAs usually arise from a letter of credit transaction (see Chapter 7). The bank sells the instrument to investors in the secondary market at a discount and accepts the responsibility for repaying the loan, thus shielding the investor from importer default risk. In the United States, most BAs are issued for less than 180 days in order to remain eligible for discount treatment at the Fed.

- *Repurchase agreements (repos).* Repos are transactions between the dealer (a securities dealer or bank investment department) and the investor. The dealer sells a security to the investor with an agreement to repurchase the security on a certain date in the future at a predetermined price, usually the next day. The custody arrangements used with repos are important in assessing the overall risk of the investment. Repos may become unsecured transactions if the investor does not have a secured interest in the collateral. In addition to the dealer risks, the investor also has the additional risk in the value of the collateral dropping below the value of the repo.

- *Sweeps.* Sweep accounts were introduced in the 1980s to overcome the Regulation Q prohibition on paying interest on corporate demand deposit accounts (see Chapter 8). Transaction balances in DDAs are swept on an overnight basis into an interest-bearing account. These balances are often maintained offshore to increase returns or are invested in overnight repos. Balances are returned to the DDA as the first transaction of the following day.

  The rate paid on sweep accounts is usually fairly low, reflecting the late notice and overnight nature of the funds. There is often a charge for a sweep account, and sometimes only the excess above a required target balance is swept. However, sweeps offer the cash manager the opportunity to earn a return on otherwise idle funds, and the rates will usually be higher than the alternative earnings credit rate (see Chapter 8).

Corporate Instruments

Although corporate obligations are considered to have a higher risk of default than government or bank instruments, many of these risks can be mitigated using credit-enhancement techniques. Some of the obligations considered to be most suitable for short-term investment portfolios are:

- *Commercial paper (CP).* Commercial paper is an unsecured promissory note, issued for a specific amount and repayable on a specific date in the future. To avoid registration with the Securities and Exchange Commission, maturities range from 1 to 270 days, although most CP is issued for 180 days or less. CP issues are often sold on a revolving basis, renewable at each maturity date. Sales are either directly to investors or through dealers, such as banks and securities companies.

- *Preferred stock.* Preferred stock allows a company to benefit from the *intercorporate dividend deduction.* Provided a stock is purchased before the ex-dividend date and is held, unhedged, for a minimum of 45 days, the corporate investor can exclude up to 70 percent of dividends received from income.

- *Money market mutual funds (MMF).* MMFs are large pools of short-term financial instruments, from which shares are sold to investors. One of the greatest benefits of MMFs is that they allow investors to earn money market yields for small individual amounts of investment. MMFs are typically highly liquid and diversified, and can respond quickly to market changes to provide investors with above-average yields.

Interest Rates

Most short-term investment issues (other than U.S. governments) are rated by one of the credit rating agencies, for example, Moody's or Standard & Poor's. The rating reflects the creditworthiness of the issuer, the amount being raised given existing debt, collateral or backup credit facilities, and the general level of interest rates. Besides the issuer default risk, a number of other factors influence the overall rate or yield on an instrument. When deciding between various investment options, the cash manager needs to convert all of the rate information to an annualized yield so that the investment options may be compared on a common basis.

After default risk, the most important factors influencing rates are:

- *Term.* Length of time to maturity. Longer-term instruments are perceived as carrying greater risk of volatility than shorter-term, due to the potential deterioration in value of the future stream of interest and the principal payments due to inflation.

- *Depth of the market.* Active markets are more attractive and investments are easier to sell than those in thinly traded markets.

- *Tax status.* Some investments are paid on a tax-free or partially tax-exempt basis. Yields must be adjusted to reflect the tax effect.

- *Yearly basis.* A year is calculated either on a 360 or 365-day basis. Short-term instruments of one year or less are often calculated on the basis of 360 days. Longer-term investments usually use 365 days. A 365-day basis provides a higher yield.

- *Discount or interest bearing.* Discount instruments will have a higher yield factor than the stated discount rate or simple interest rate.

- *Compounding or simple interest.* Instruments that compound interest have a higher effective yield than simple interest investments.

Issues in Short-term Investing

The cash manager has three objectives when investing funds in short-term instruments:

1. *Retaining value.* Protecting the principal amount is the primary objective of a cash manager. Temporary short-term surpluses need to be invested in instruments that have little or no risk of losing value. The company's investment policy will specify acceptable instruments and level of risk. Most cash managers will be conservative in investing liquidity reserves.

2. *Raising cash quickly.* The second objective of short-term investing is to ensure that there is sufficient liquidity to cover the company's financial obligations. This means having a reserve of assets that can be converted into cash, quickly and without significant loss in value. To accomplish this objective, the market has to be active and deep, that is, with many buyers and sellers at any moment in time.

High-risk Investment

In 1994, Robert Citron, the ex-treasurer for Orange County in California, made headlines by investing the county's liquidity funds in high-risk, volatile derivative instruments. Their lack of liquidity cost the county $1.7 billion, plunging it into bankruptcy. The irony is that, eventually, the investments returned a handsome profit. However, derivatives are an inappropriate vehicle for liquidity reserves.

3. *Realizing income.* The third objective is to optimize the return on any short-term surpluses. Investment guidelines will identify the level of risk that a company is prepared to trade off for higher returns.

Investment Policies

Most companies have written policies that clearly define the parameters of acceptable risks, instruments, counterparties, and maturities for investments. These guidelines establish a company's position between risk aversion and profit potential. Each company will have a different profile, reflecting its appetite for risk and expectations on return.

A committee made up of senior managers will normally draft an investment policy. Exhibit 5.5 outlines the issues that an investment policy should address. There should also be a provision for a periodic review of the policy to reflect current market conditions and board of directors' concerns.

Passive and Active Strategies

A cash manager can choose to take a passive or active approach to managing short-term investments.

EXHIBIT 5.5

Investment Policy Guidelines

Investment objective
What is the company's acceptable level of risk and yield, and in particular, the importance of yield given the safety of principal and liquidity?

Investment authority
Who within the company is authorized to implement the above policy, make investments on behalf of the company; and to what limits and in which instruments?

Audit trails
What type and frequency of reporting and audit trails will be required to monitor compliance with the investment policy?

Permitted or restricted instruments
Which investment instruments (bank, corporate, or government issues) are permitted or prohibited in the portfolio? What is the accepted credit quality and marketability?

Maturity
Which maturities are acceptable in terms of risk and liquidity?

Diversification of investments
What are the maximum allowable positions in different types of investments, with regard to issuers, industry, and country of issuer?

Counterparties
Who are the acceptable dealers and issuers with whom the company is prepared to deal, and in what amounts?

Safekeeping
What custodial arrangements are required, both to safeguard the company's investment and to facilitate audit requirements?

- A *passive strategy*, often used by smaller companies, involves matching maturities to the timing of when funds will be needed; or using a sweep account, where the funds are invested automatically on an overnight basis. Both of these approaches are very conservative and may not maximize investment returns.

- An *active strategy,* used by larger companies, can increase yield. However, there is more risk to the principal, as well as higher costs. An example of an active strategy is riding the yield curve, which involves mismatching the maturity date to the time when funds will be needed to take advantage of the differences in rates at varying maturities.

Exhibit 5.6 illustrates two types of yield curves: a normal curve, where interest rates rise as the maturity date extends; and an inverted yield curve, where interest rates are higher in the short term than in the long term.

Inverted yield curves are usually short-lived and self-correcting, although in recent times there have been examples of inverted yield curves lasting for more than a year. Using an active approach to investment in a normal curve environment, a cash manager with a temporary surplus for six months can place the money for one year to earn the higher rate of interest, and then sell after six months. In an inverted yield curve market, the cash manager will place the funds for one month and keep reinvesting through the six-month period.

EXHIBIT 5.6

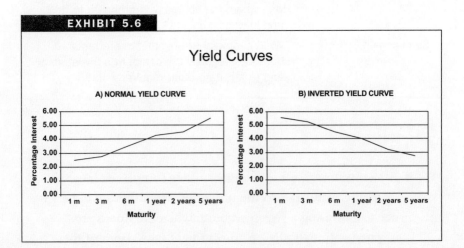

110

Surplus Cash

The majority of small to medium-sized companies find that sweeps are the most cost-effective way to invest surplus cash. Active management is both time-consuming and expensive. Sweeps have a small administrative monthly charge (usually $100 to $150) and are an entirely automated bank service. Before making any investment decisions, the cash manager must determine whether this is really the best use of the funds. Paying down debt may be a better use of temporary surpluses.

In both cases, the strategy is most successful if the market is stable and the shape of the yield curve constant. In the first example—the normal curve—there is a danger that if interest rates rise, the price (and liquidation value) of the instrument will fall. In the second example—the inverted yield curve—the cash manager may find that when it is time to reinvest the funds the curve has normalized and short-terms rates are lower than the long-term rates.

Borrowing

The cash manager's responsibilities include ensuring that there are sufficient unused borrowing facilities in place to cover any temporary shortfalls in working capital. These facilities are an essential part of the liquidity management equation.

The need to borrow will be influenced by seasonal factors, the timing of cash flows, and general business conditions. If the cash forecasting of these elements has been accurate, the cash manager will be positioned to make arrangements well in advance and at favorable terms.

In addition to arranging for adequate credit to be available, the cash manager has also to ensure that the terms are not onerous as to restrictions and covenants, and that the cost is reasonable. Just as the cash manager has many options to consider in investing funds, there are a large number of choices for funding. The optimal selection depends on the exact requirements and use of the funds.

Lines of Credit

The most important form of borrowing facility is a bank line of credit. The borrower has access to a defined amount of money over a specific period of time. The cost of a credit line depends on a number of factors, primarily the bank's assessment of the company's financial health and the overall level of interest rates.

The characteristics of a line of credit are:

- *Unsecured or secured.* In order to reduce assessed risk and, consequently, the cost of a line of credit, the lender might require some form of collateral, such as a company's accounts receivable. Unsecured lines are uncollateralized and are, therefore, more expensive.

- *Committed or uncommitted.* With a committed line of credit, the lender is obligated to make the funds available upon demand as long as the borrower meets all the conditions and terms of the agreement. An uncommitted line is a less formal agreement, with the lender under no obligation to make funds available when requested. Uncommitted lines are best used for occasional needs and for very short periods when other sources of funding are also available. An uncommitted line will be less expensive than a committed one, which will often include a commitment fee payable whether the line is used or not.

- *Revolving.* The borrower can continuously borrow and repay up to the credit limit during the life of the loan.

- *Clean-up period.* Because lines of credit are intended for use as short-term funds, lenders often require that loans be repaid in their entirety for one or two months, called the "clean-up period." This is to prove that credit lines are not being used as part of the company's long-term funding.

Other Credit Facilities

Other sources of short-term credit include:

- *Commercial paper (CP).* A company that has a sufficiently high credit rating can go directly to the money market to issue commercial paper. CP is a promissory note issued for a specific amount for a period ranging from 1 to 270 days. Publicly traded issues are usually rated by the major credit rating agencies; privately placed CP is not. Costs of CP include the broker/dealer fee and the expense for any credit enhancement, such as a standby letter of credit.

- *Asset-based financing.* When unsecured lending is not feasible, companies have a variety of asset-based borrowing to consider. Usually, the lender will finance only a percentage of the value of the assets. There are two major types of asset-based financing:

  1. *Accounts receivable.* Accounts receivables may be used for asset-based financing, commonly known as *factoring,* with or without recourse.
     - *With recourse.* The lender provides financing on the receivable and collects from the customer. If the customer defaults, the borrowing company is liable for that portion of the loan. The cost is low because the borrower accepts all risk. The factor pays the borrower about 95 percent of the billed price, collects 100 percent, and keeps the difference as a fee for the loan.
     - *Without recourse.* The lender collects from the customer and accepts the risk of default. The effective cost of the

loan is considerably higher because the lender has assumed significantly greater risk.

2. *Inventory financing.* Loans are secured by the pledge of inventory. One specialized type of inventory financing is floor planning, which is used to support the inventory of dealers who sell high-ticket durable goods, such as farming equipment and automobiles.

- *Asset-backed securities.* Securitization can help a company obtain inexpensive credit and improve its financial ratios by providing off-balance sheet financing. A pool of receivables with a predictable cash flow (e.g., mortgages, loans, leases) can be used to support the issuance of debt securities. The cash flow pays the interest charges and is used to retire the security issue. Asset-backed securities are less expensive than bank loans and broaden the market for a company's debt. However, there are various costs in using securitization: attorneys and accountants to prepare the agreements and filings; investment bankers to place the transaction; and income servicers to collect payments and remit to investors.

Cost of Borrowing

The factors that influence the final cost of borrowing include:

- *Credit risk.* The perceived risk of default by the borrower will determine the interest cost at which a lender will lend funds.

- *Rate basis.* Loans are often priced as a spread above a certain index rate. Some of the common index rates used are the prime rate (traditionally the rate at which U.S. banks lend money to their most creditworthy clients), the London Interbank Rate (LIBOR, set in London on a daily basis), or federal funds (the rate at which commercial banks lend excess reserves to each other, as set by the Federal Reserve).

- *Fixed or variable.* Depending on current and expected future

TIPS & TECHNIQUES

Exploring Internal Sources of Funds

Before borrowing from external sources, a cash manager should also explore all internal sources of funds. These could include increasing sales, accelerating accounts receivable and collections, reducing inventory, improving accounts payable management, reducing expenses, and selling nonessential assets.

market conditions, a rate can be fixed for the entire time of the loan or be adjusted at regular intervals.

- *Tax basis.* Interest paid on debt is usually deductible from income, reducing the effective overall cost of debt.

- *Annual basis.* 360 or 365. A 365 basis will result in a higher cost of debt.

- *Maturity.* Under normal yield curve conditions, borrowers will pay more for longer-term debt.

- *Discount or interest-bearing.* Discount instruments result in less available funds at the outset of the loan but an equivalent amount of interest paid over the life of the instrument.

- *Secured or unsecured.* Collateralized borrowing will result in lower fees.

- *Credit enhancement.* The cost of adding a backup line of credit or standby letter of credit can add significant cost to the financing.

- *Credit rating.* The issuing company pays the cost of the credit rating valuation.

- *Other fees and costs.* Many instruments have additional dealer or broker fees. Some banks will require an interest-free compensating balance.

The cash manager must factor in all of the elements that impact the cost of borrowing to make a fair assessment of the total cost of short-term debt.

Summary

Managing liquidity is vital to a company's financial health. The first step is to find an appropriate forecasting system, suitable for the business and for the time horizon. The type of information that is readily and reliably available will also govern the selection. The more accurately the cash manager is able to analyze historical trends and project them in the light of the current environment, the better prepared the company will be to manage excesses when they occur and to fund shortfalls when necessary.

CASE STUDY

Ann developed a series of short-term forecasts to help her better manage the centralized liquidity in the company. By estimating the shortfalls for GETDOE's seasonal businesses, she is now able to cover the deficits in the cash-poor divisions with excess cash in others. She was also able to put lines of credit in place at acceptable terms to cover the eventuality of a shortfall. To her surprise, Ann discovered that the company had excess temporary surpluses that are now being invested according to the policy developed by Bill and the management committee.

CHAPTER 6

Treasury Information Systems

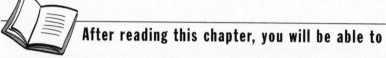

After reading this chapter, you will be able to

- Understand how treasury information systems are used to expedite the communication between the bank and the company

- Review features, benefits, and disadvantages of treasury workstations and Internet-based systems

- Develop a coherent strategy for the selection of a treasury information system

CASE STUDY

Treasurer Bill Fold and Cash Manager Ann I. Shade were informed by their bankers that the collection, concentration, and disbursement systems they selected require access through a treasury information system. Ann was familiar with electronic banking platforms and had used them at her previous company. Until now, GETDOE had assumed that the cost of these systems could not be justified. However, the move to a centralized treasury and the security concerns expressed by the external auditors meant that Ann must reassess treasury workstation alternatives. Bill and Ann have a number of options to consider.

The old economy of industrial production, materials, and labor has transitioned in the past decade to a new economy of information and finance. As recently as 1980 the cash manager could obtain only limited daily balance and transaction data from banks. Originally, the information was transmitted through a "dumb terminal" dial-up to bank computer systems or by telephone. Once data was polled and printed, the cash manager entered the numbers onto a worksheet to calculate the next day's estimated cash position. The "new economy" treasurer has access to various financial delivery systems, including a full range of current-day bank information.

In considering opportunities to improve the efficiency of treasury information management, it is important to remember that each company has differing information requirements. Some treasurers require only the basic data—how much was deposited, which checks cleared, and what are the current ledger and available balances. Small and medium-sized companies can obtain these data by accessing recorded telephone menus and hand recording each day's results. Large, decentralized companies may need highly sophisticated information systems, with numerous modules and services. The various options are reviewed in the next section.

Treasury Information Modules

A treasury information system allows a company to electronically access its bank accounts and transaction activity. The two prevalent system configurations involve PC-based systems, often referred to as a *treasury workstation* (TWS), and Internet-based systems, accessed through a Web browser. The largest companies often choose to establish mainframe-to-mainframe computer interfaces.

The Basic Modules

The following modules provide the basic reporting required by many companies. The technology for these systems is available from most banks, several of which have a long history of product development and delivery.

- *Previous-day and same-day reporting.* Yesterday's and today's ledger and available balances are listed, including details of debits and credits, float by day (zero-, one-, and two-day), and other transactions. There is usually a premium charge for same-day reporting. Since banks run their DDA systems (from which much of this information is derived) overnight, same-day reporting requires feeds from separate reporting systems and is, therefore, more costly to develop.

- *Polling and parsing.* Account data can be retrieved by *polling* banks electronically and then downloading or *parsing* information into reports based on a script developed at the time of installation. Important features include the following:

  - Automatic dialing of banks
  - Electronic responses through scripts
  - Selection of appropriate data
  - Formatting into reports
  - Exception reports of banks for which information was unavailable

- *Domestic wire transfer.* As discussed in Chapter 2, wire transfers are same-day, final transfers primarily used for large dollar transactions. Current practice for control and security strongly encourages these transactions be initiated through a bank's proprietary software (rather than by telephone or fax), using keys and passwords unique to the sender and receiver.

- *ACH.* Many banks now offer terminal-based ACH, allowing debit and credit transfers to be initiated by treasury rather than through the mainframe computer system.

- *Controlled disbursement.* Information modules offer various electronic reporting options, including stop payments, the transmission of checks-issued files (for positive pay review and

monthly reconciliation), the review of positive pay mismatches, and the initiation of funding wires, book transfers, or
ACHs to cover the daily cleared amount. (See Chapter 4 for
additional explanation.)

- *Multibank reporting.* Several treasury information systems can
  consolidate basic balance and transaction activity from a company's banking network, simplifying the task and reducing the
  cost of retrieving these data each day from each bank.

- *Bank relationship management.* A useful module is information
  on each bank relationship and contact, including:

  - Name, address, telephone, and fax numbers

  - Names of senior managers, calling officers, and cus-
    tomer service staff

  - History of the relationship and calling efforts

  - Listing of services used, persistent problems, and unique
    characteristics

  - Credit facilities available and used, as well as fees,
    restrictions, and loan covenants

Other Modules

The largest dozen or so banks offer additional modules, designed to
meet the needs of global corporations.

- *Foreign exchange (FX).* Banks offer modules to expedite the
  process of purchasing or selling foreign currency, primarily in
  the major currencies used in international transactions: the euro,
  the Japanese yen, and the British pound, as well as the currencies of the other NAFTA countries, the Mexican peso, and the
  Canadian dollar. Other currencies may be available based on the
  market presence of each bank and the requirements of its corporate customers. In addition to automating FX transactions,
  these modules usually offer lower transaction charges and better
  rates than polling financial institutions by telephone.

- *Letters of credit.* Export and import financing usually requires bank letters of credit to assure payment once all documentation and other requirements have been completed. Letters of credit (LC) modules enable automated processing of the LC and supporting documentation.

- *International money transfer.* The movement of funds between banks in different countries involves linking various different international money transfer systems, usually using SWIFT formats (see Chapter 2).

- *Investment management.* The management of portfolios of investments can be simplified by tracking short- and long-term holdings, including trades, mark-to-market pricing, and the tracking of dividends, interest, and option income.

- *Debt management.* Debt modules typically report commercial paper activity, fixed- and floating-rate instruments, credit line activity, and intercompany loans.

- *Pooling and netting.* Pooling is a technique used by in-house banks (often domiciled in treasury centers) to offset the deficits in the accounts of certain subsidaries with excess cash in the accounts of other subsidiaries. In addition to the daily aggregation of account balances, interest debits and credits are calculated and periodically paid based on parameters established by the company. Netting involves the reduction in the number of intracompany payments through the consolidation and aggregation of individual transactions. (See Chapter 7 for further explanation.)

Treasury Workstations

The term *treasury workstation* generally refers to a self-contained bank- or vendor-supported treasury information system. The software that supports the system resides on a stand-alone PC or on a network-based computer system, and is comprised of modules that provide some or all of the functionalities described in the previous section. In addition, the software package requires telephone modem access for automated dial-up and access to bank databases containing transactional activity, and sequencing for specific functions.

The early treasury workstation products provided important features not previously available from dumb terminals. However, there were several deficiencies that affected the efficiency of treasury staff:

- Repetitive keying was required to move between modules and other systems.

- Company-specific spreadsheets had to be created.

- Few analytical tools were provided within the bank systems.

Advanced Functionality

Banks and vendors wishing to remain competitive in this market have developed various advanced functions:

- Interfacing to various databases

  - External financial data (such as Bloomberg, Telerate, Reuters, and EDGAR)

  - Internal accounting data, including the general ledger and budget reports

  - Internal financial data, including cash schedules and forecasts

  - Other internal systems linkages, including receivables, payables, and enterprise resource planning (ERP) configurations

- Mapping of repetitive transactions to automate journal entries

- Reconciling bank and book balances

- Testing the impact of what-if scenarios on the cash position

- Customized report writing to present data that has been assembled and analyzed

- Converting raw data files to spreadsheet files or other formats

These elements are shown in Exhibit 6.1, a schematic of an integrated treasury management system. The circles represent the interconnected nature of the various modules, with management reporting derived as a function of the collective informational content of the inputs.

The central cash management system is supported by live data from sales (for receivables) and purchases (for payables), with feeds to accounting for recurring cash-related transactions, whenever and wherever they occur, and occasional treasury "deals." Exhibit 6.2 provides the company and product names of leading treasury workstations. In addi-

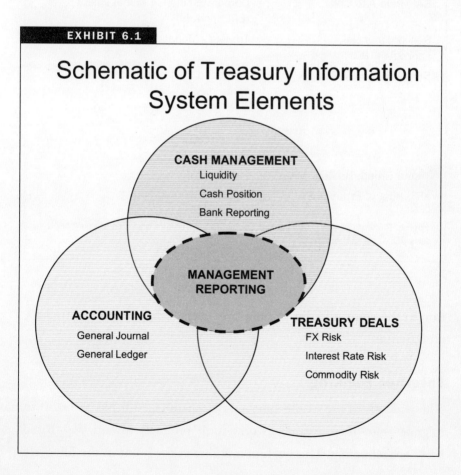

EXHIBIT 6.1

Schematic of Treasury Information System Elements

CASH MANAGEMENT
Liquidity
Cash Position
Bank Reporting

MANAGEMENT REPORTING

ACCOUNTING
General Journal
General Ledger

TREASURY DEALS
FX Risk
Interest Rate Risk
Commodity Risk

EXHIBIT 6.2

Products of Leading Treasury Workstation Vendors

Company and Location	Products
Gateway Systems, Barrington, IL	Xpress Treasury Management System Global Treasury Management System
Integrity Treasury Solutions, Chicago, IL	Integra-T
Peoplesoft, Pleasanton, CA	ERP modules
SAP, Palo Alto CA	Corporate Finance Management (ERP module)
Selkirk Financial, Vancouver, BC	Treasury Manager
Sungard, Calabasas, CA	Advanced Portfolio Systems, ETreasury GTM ICMS ResourceQ2 Quantum
Trema Group, Boston, MA	Finance KIT
XRT, King of Prussia, PA	Treasury Workstation

Source: Richard Gamble, "Making the Connection," *Treasury and Risk Management,* June 2001, pp. 31–40.

tion to the companies listed, there are several other vendors of treasury workstations.

Internet Banking

The widespread use of the Internet has encouraged banks to begin to migrate from their treasury workstation products toward Web-based browser technology. This evolution comes at the point in the life cycle of the treasury information system, when banks have begun to generally back away from full product support of sophisticated technology. This development is due both to the cost of the expertise and equipment and to the difficulty of keeping products current with rapidly evolving customer demands.

Bank Internet-based systems are accessed through a standard Web browser, making the full range of treasury services available at any time and in all locations. The user is no longer tied to a specific PC loaded with the bank's proprietary software. This allows treasury managers who are away from their offices to access their bank position and execute transactions from any computer. Another advantage is that users throughout a large company can access specific modules and make financial decisions.

The market penetration of the product has been impressive, with more than one-fourth of all corporate customers receiving treasury information services through an Internet banking product by early in 2001 (as reported in the Ernst & Young Cash Management Survey). Some 85 percent of

IN THE REAL WORLD

An Advantage of Internet Banking

As one example, accounts payable staff can review positive pay files directly to determine if check mismatches should be honored or rejected. In the workstation situation, this process was handled by treasury staff, who were often uninformed as to the purpose or validity of a particular disbursement. The result was a series of telephone calls, e-mails, or faxes, and any delay meant that the period for review (usually only about four hours) had passed. In that situation, the bank decision reverts to the preset accept or reject blanket rule made by the company at the time the account was established; that default is almost always "accept."

financial institutions providing such services are now offering Internet delivery, and nearly all banks will be offering Internet delivery exclusively or together with a workstation (at least in the short run). Exhibit 6.3 con-

---

EXHIBIT 6.3

Internet-based Treasury Information Systems from U.S. Banks

Bank	Development Stage
ABN-AMRO LaSalle Bank	Full
Allfirst Bank	Partial
AmSouth	Full
Bank of America	Full
Bank One	Partial
Bank of New York	Full
Citibank	In development
First Union	Partial
Fleet Boston	Partial
Harris Bank/Bank of Montreal	Partial
J.P. Morgan Chase	Full
Huntington Bank	Partial
KeyBank	Partial
Mellon Bank	In development
National City Bank	In development
Northern Trust	Full
PNC Bank	Partial
SunTrust Bank	Full
Wachovia Bank	Full
Wells Fargo	Full

Full: The offering of a full range of information services.
Partial: Certain basic services are available, with others under development.

Note: Many of these banks are using the technology offered by third-party providers, such as Politizer and HANEY, and Magnet.
Source: Richard Gamble, "Do Banks Really Want Your Business?" Treasury and Risk Management, March 2001, pp. 36–44; updated in "Corporate Strings Attached," April 2002, p. 34.

tains a representative listing of Internet-based systems offered by U.S. banks. The Tower Group estimates that over half of all coporate users will be accessing Web-based services by 2005.

Benefits

There are various advantages to the use of Internet-based services:

- *Cost.* A full range of modules is available to users at nominal cost. Automating bank transactions greatly reduces bank costs for personnel, technology, and customer service, and brings a suite of treasury services previously unavailable to many medium-sized and smaller corporations.

- *Single-platform access.* Access through a single platform allows the corporate user to move easily from one product to another. While some treasury workstation products are similarly orga-nized, others have separate dial-ups, log-ons, security proce-dures, and screen designs for various cash management modules.

- *Easy implementation.* New modules can be added with minimal setup, delivery effort, and cost. User-friendly menus enable users to quickly learn and adopt new technology.

- *Ease of upgrading software.* In a treasury workstation environ-ment, software must be physically installed on each PC, result-ing in multiple installations each time software is upgraded. On the Web this is accomplished easily with updates being loaded onto a single server.

- *Straight-through processing.* Vendors can begin to focus efforts on straight-through or full-cycle processing, involving entire sec-tions of the cash flow timeline. For example, e-commerce pur-chasing, accounts payable, and disbursement services are becoming available as banks look to expand their product offerings and as companies outsource functions not considered as core competencies.

- *Pricing.* Fees for Internet-based products are lower than bank workstations and significantly less than for vendor-supported treasury workstations. Depending on the configuration, bank workstations typically cost in the low five figures, often in the $25,000 range. Vendor workstations can cost $50,000 for the minimal configuration, and as much as $500,000 for full functionality. Internet-based treasury information services may cost a few thousand dollars per module.

Disadvantages

Disadvantages include the following:

- *Noncore competency.* Many banks would prefer not to allocate the required capital or expertise to the design and maintenance of an Internet-based product. The delivery system is significantly more complex than merely loading software onto a disk and having the corporate customer dial into the bank's computer. For example, banks have been forced to hire network engineers to create and support the required telecommunications infrastructure.

- *Technology issues.* The receipt of bank information is typically slower by Internet than through treasury workstations. This is often due to the use of low-speed data connections and the limitations of common carrier bandwidth, inadequate PC systems, and corporate firewalls established to deter hackers and viruses.

  - Computer systems, telecommunications, and software may need to be upgraded to optimize information exchange.

  - Companies will have to work with IT and security staffs to overcome firewall problems while preserving a reasonable level of internal security. Controls will be required on users not previously allowed access to treasury information to prevent unauthorized actions. These new users include personnel from outside of treasury and treasury users attempting remote access by laptop or home PCs.

- *Security.* Concern for security has been an ongoing issue with all Internet users due to the potential for hacking and for virus infections.

  - Hackers are intrusions involving illegal listening on data transmissions, and may result in the theft or fraudulent use of proprietary company information.

  - Viruses involve lines of code inserted into computer programs to modify and possibly destroy data and software. The virus often replicates itself to spread through an entire computer network.

  Current versions of Internet-based treasury information services operate in secure environments with minimal risk of the loss or destruction of data.

  - Secure private networks operate between the provider and the bank.

  - Protected 128-bit encrypted Web channels operate between the bank and the corporate customer. These communication networks utilize digital certificates, password protection, and challenge responses to identify and admit the user.

  Still, the prevailing attitude among auditors and information technology staff remains sufficiently negative that security problems continue to be an obstacle when considering Internet-based systems.

Internet-banking and the Service Providers

Banks and their corporate customers have learned some expensive lessons in attempting to support their treasury information system products while providing the enhancements demanded by corporate users.

- *Technical support.* Traditional treasury workstation software resides on the client server, and is managed from that site. Any time the system crashes, or whenever there is a technology problem or an upgrade has to be installed, the banks are expected to provide the necessary service at low or no charge. Contemporary practice is for so-called thin client architecture, with applications managed at the provider's site. This approach greatly simplifies the effort required for technical support.

- *Pricing.* System design and support involves significant development and maintenance costs, which go far beyond the usual treasury management fee of a few cents (i.e., the check clearing charge) to a few dollars (i.e., the Fedwire charge) per transaction. The current trend is to use private-branded treasury systems supported by independent software developers.

Nonbank vendors have entered the market with sophisticated, multifunctional products, including treasury modules as integral components of ERP systems (see Chapter 10). In partnership with the large accounting and consulting firms, these vendors provide assistance in the determination of requirements, integration with legacy systems, interface with the general ledger, user training, and implementation. Comprehensive services are provided that banks cannot support.

Many banks have decided to focus on their core businesses of lending and cash management, and have rejected the vendor/ERP/consulting partnership model. Instead, they have choosen to deliver Internet-based treasury information services created and maintained by specialized vendors, but under their own logo and private label. The largest of these vendors are Politzer and HANEY, and Magnet.

- Politzer and HANEY (Newtown, Massachusetts) offers its products through Allfirst Bank, AmSouth, Bank One, Citibank, J.P. Morgan Chase, Merrill Lynch, Wells Fargo, and various regional and smaller institutions.

- Magnet (Atlanta, Georgia) cites various banks, including ABN-AMRO LaSalle Bank, Bank of America, Harris Bank/Bank of Montreal, National City, SunTrust, and several regional and smaller institutions.

Choosing a Treasury Information System

The implementation of a treasury information system should be constructed as a multiphase inquiry, with each step logically following from the conclusions reached in the previous investigatory step.

Step 1: Determine Information Requirements

Deciding on a treasury information system should begin with the determination of the company's requirements, particularly in the context of the current use of data and any perceived deficiencies. How is treasury data currently being developed? Are there problems with the timing, quality, or information content of the results? Some useful questions to consider include the following:

- What time of day does the company typically know/need to know its cash position?
- How many telephone calls or other bank contacts are required to develop these data?
- Are the system and connections to accounting and financial interfaces primarily manual, involving internal company communications and the rekeying of data?
- Have several significant mistakes or missed borrowing/investing opportunities occurred in the past year?
- Is the company employing more treasury staff than peer group companies?
- Have banks and/or accountants repeatedly been suggesting increasing the automation of the treasury information system?

Many companies find that an ad hoc project team is useful in developing answers to these questions. The team should represent functions likely to be affected by any decision on a new system, including treasury, finance, accounting, and information technology. The answers to these questions should drive the decision as to whether to proceed to step 2.

Step 2: Conduct Vendor Search

Several venues provide competitive information on bank and vendor products. These include the following:

- *Treasury conferences.* The most important exhibition for banks and vendors is the Association of Financial Professionals (AFP) Annual Conference, which meets every autumn in a major U.S. city. In 2003, the meeting will be held in Orlando, November 9–12; in 2004, Boston, October 24–27; and in 2005, San Antonio, October 9–12. The number of exhibitors at this event is about 250, perhaps one-third of which offer some form of treasury information system product.

- *Others.* Regional cash management associations offer some exhibitor space. The largest of these regional meetings include:
  - The New York Cash Exchange, held in early September
  - The Windy City (Chicago), held in late May
  - Expo LA (southern California), held in late April or May

- *Print and Internet media.* The various print media offer both advertising for systems and periodic directory listings; names and Web site addresses are listed here:

TIPS & TECHNIQUES

Benefits Outweigh Costs

Although the cost of attendance at a treasury conference can be $2,000 or more, including registration fees, hotel, and transportation, the opportunity to see and compare systems in one central venue is likely to be more cost-effective than separate visits to or by competing vendors. In addition, there are over 100 sessions offered on various aspects of treasury and financial management, keynote speakers, and other eduational activities.

- AFP publications, including *AFP Exchange, AFP Pulse,* and numerous others (*www.afponline.org*)
- *Treasury and Risk Management* (*www.treasuryandrisk.com*)
- *Business Finance* (*www.businessfinance.com*)
- *The Treasurer* (U.K.) (*www.treasurers.org*)
- *Global Treasury News* (U.K.) (*www.gtnews.com*)

Banks and vendors should be contacted for detailed information on treasury information system offerings, including modules, hardware requirements, implementation support, and typical pricing. The responses should be reviewed for compatibility with your requirements, and a ranking should be developed to focus on no more than three or four candidate systems.

Step 3: Review Vendor Offerings

The company's requirements should be matched against the system specifications provided by the selected banks and vendors. Consideration should be given to such issues as customer service, hardware requirements, implementation time and support, reputation and financial strength, commitment to the business, comments by references, and pricing. Pricing includes various vendor and internal components, and these should be carefully estimated to determine the fully loaded cost of the new system:

- Initial fees, including start-up costs and site preparation
- Training
- Implementation fees
- Maintenance fees
- Technology upgrades, including hardware and telecommunications
- Ongoing internal support

A scoring matrix can be developed to assist in evaluating proposals received in response to your request-for-proposal (RFP). (The AFP offers a treasury workstation RFP in its publication *Standardized RFPs, Volume 2*). Finalists should be visited to meet the team assigned to support your company and to ask questions regarding future vendor strategies. Site visits to current users are often helpful, particularly to discuss operating issues, problems, and bank or vendor support with the staff actually using the workstation.

Step 4: Provide Economic Justification

Traditional economic analysis is not likely to be of much assistance in making the decision on a treasury information system. There are three important benefits from a workstation or Internet system that are difficult to subject to a capital budgeting analysis:

1. *The quality of the information available to the treasury manager.* Rather than receiving raw data, treasury has the opportunity to view a variety of data feeds organized in a logical report presentation.

2. *The opportunity for rationalization of bank account structures and treasury files, documents, and processes.* As the result of better bank account information, management can eliminate idle or redundant accounts, determine if adequate controls are in place to safeguard cash and other financial assets, and compare banking costs across all financial institutions.

3. *The general business process efficiencies gained through the improvement of existing practices.* The installation of the new treasury information system encourages an examination of the cash flow timeline and the reengineering or outsourcing of selected activities.

The quantifiable savings are likely to be in time saved in polling banks for details of daily activity, in entering data into a spreadsheet or database, in such clerical functions as reconciling book and bank account balances, and in arriving at a final cash position for investing or borrowing decisions. The total time saving is not likely to be more than three to four hours daily, and that time may be a fixed charge if the treasury analyst is a full-time position.

Step 5: Choose the System

The greatest challenge in the final choice of a treasury information system may be in balancing the functionality, the cost, and the commitment of the bank or vendor to the service. However, whether a treasury workstation or an Internet product is selected, the following issues should be addressed:

- Who will service and maintain the product: the bank, the vendor, or the third-party Internet provider? Will the service be available 24/7 or only during normal business hours? Is the product supported by technology experts or by customer service staff who respond to menu-driven questions?

IN THE REAL WORLD

Reasons Companies Are Choosing Internet-based Banking

Many companies today are opting for an Internet-based service, because of several factors:

- The partnership of a financial institution and a specialized Internet vendor

- The convenience of access through any PC or laptop

- The assurance of security and control

- The relatively low expense of acquiring and maintaining the technology

- The ease of exiting from the relationship without a significant sunk cost in acquiring software or hardware upgrades

- What happens in the event of a system failure or disaster? Does the bank or vendor have adequate, secure backup facilities?
- Does the bank or vendor have a reasonable number of references from satisfied customers?
- Is there any concern for compatibility with other treasury and accounting systems?
- Is the product user-friendly, or will extensive training be required?
- What is the commitment of the bank or vendor to the business? How long are they likely to continue to offer support and improve the product?

Summary

Treasury information systems offer a variety of modules for manipulating and managing cash. The treasurer faces two delivery system choices: the treasury workstation and Internet-based systems. The decision on modules and the delivery system is usually based on comfort and compatibility with the technology and on the alternatives offered by the primary banking relationship. Companies too often choose a treasury information system without carefully reviewing necessary internal processing improvements and uses of data, which is a critical first step in the process.

CASE STUDY

Bill and Ann understood that they would require a reliable, inexpensive, and supported treasury information system to access their banking relationships. Of the options available, the most attractive appeared to be an Internet-based system. However, they also realized that some work would first be necessary to determine their requirements and internal changes to adjust to the new technology.

CHAPTER 7

International Cash Management

After reading this chapter, you will be able to

- Identify the complexities of international cash management
- Evaluate the risks associated with cross–border transactions
- Assess the major tools and organizational structures used to improve global cash flows
- Understand how developments in Europe impact liquidity management
- Review tips for treasurers with emerging international business

CASE STUDY

The treasurer of GETDOE, Bill Fold, has just been advised of the acquisition of a large Western European manufacturer and distributor. This follows the outsourcing of some U.S. manufacturing to Mexico two years earlier. Until now Bill has supervised a U.S. dollar-based business, supplemented with occasional foreign exchange contracts. The European acquisition, with its euro and British pound-based businesses, means that the structure of treasury and how it controls overseas cash flows will have to be totally reexamined for issues such as:

- *Identifying the new risks associated with the international operations*

- *Deciding how to mitigate any resulting exposures*

- *Determining how to optimally manage liquidity*

- *Establishing a new banking structure to better meet the company's future needs.*

The new global company will have to be organized very differently from the old, domestically focused one. To help him bridge the knowledge gap, Bill hired Rick Shaw as international cash manager to assist in determining and implementing the new structure. Rick had previously been with one of the major banks, consulting with clients on global liquidity management. His challenge will be to apply his vast product knowledge and international banking experience to the real world of the corporate environment.

F
ew companies today can entirely escape the impact of globalization. Even the smallest companies find that they are buying, sourcing, and selling internationally or facing competition from abroad. Cash managers are moving beyond their domestic responsibilities and taking on the complexities of managing international funds flows.

The Growth of International Business

Mastering the challenges of international risk and liquidity management requires new skills and a much broader knowledge of how business is transacted in other countries. Considering the inefficiencies of some international markets, it also opens up new areas of opportunity for treasury to make a significant contribution to company profitability. In the United States, float is measured in fractions of a day; internationally, it extends to several weeks.

International business was traditionally the domain of multinational companies, but since the advent of the Internet and the globalizing

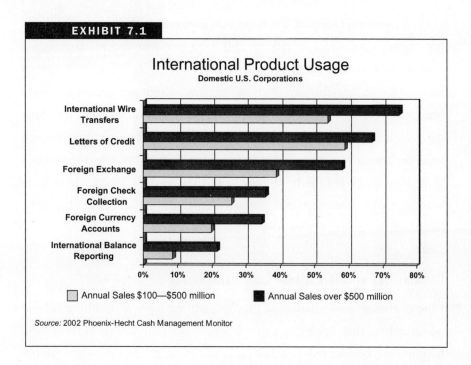

EXHIBIT 7.1

International Product Usage
Domestic U.S. Corporations

Source: 2002 Phoenix-Hecht Cash Management Monitor

economy, this is no longer the case. Exhibit 7.1 illustrates the range of international banking products and services large and middle-market companies are using.

The International Treasury Environment

The objectives of international cash management are fundamentally the same as for domestic cash management: accelerate collections, control disbursements, and use any excess cash optimally. Achieving these goals requires timely and accurate information, and tools to facilitate the efficient movement of funds. However, this is much more difficult to achieve in a global context. The objective of international cash management can be described as:

> Having the right *currency,* in the right *place,* at the right *time,* with the right *information.*

The interpretation of the objective, however, will vary according to a company's tolerance of risk, its ability to monitor and manage exposure, and its trading patterns. A company with limited foreign currency receivables and payables, or with an inability to manage exposure, might prefer to have all currencies concentrated in U.S. dollars. Another company with high volumes of two-way foreign currency flows may choose to maintain currency accounts overseas for convenience, lower transaction costs, and use of natural hedges. In the world of international cash management, *managing and limiting exposure,* rather than liquidity, becomes the primary objective.

Complexities of International Cash Management

One of the greatest challenges for the cash manager is dealing with the complexities that arise from the different ways in which business and banking are conducted in other parts of the world. Some of the factors that need to be considered are:

- Cultural Differences
    - Holidays, weekends, and religious practices
    - Payment method preferences
    - Usual trade payment terms
    - Expected tone, format, and setting for business discussions
    - Dating conventions
- Economic and Monetary Environment
    - Foreign exchange rate fluctuations
    - Local interest and inflation rates
- Banking Practices
    - Banking structure and central bank control
    - Permitted account opening and signing authority

- Treatment of nonresident and foreign currency accounts
- Standard bank compensation practices (discussed later)
- Banking practice in terms of interest on checking accounts, overdraft banking, and overnight investment vehicles

- Communications Infrastructure
  - Level of technology and communications infrastructure
  - Ease of cross-border communications
  - Availability of hardware and software
  - Degree of automation in business

- Legal and Regulatory Environment
  - Presence of exchange control regulations
  - Requirements for central bank documentation
  - Secrecy law restrictions
  - Restrictions on nonresident banking activities
  - Restrictions on local and cross-border liquidity management tools

- Tax Implications
  - Extent of tax treaties and double taxation agreements
  - Treatment of intercompany loans
  - Stamp duties and other taxes on banking activities
  - Existence of tax-advantaged international treasury vehicles

- Time Zones—impact on liquidity management, payment initiation, and customer service

- Language Barriers
  - Account opening and other legal documents in local language

- Impact on customer service issues
- Cultural differences and nuances of use of language that may inhibit or preclude comprehension

Bank Compensation Practices

Although many countries charge on a transaction basis, as in the United States, paying through balances is almost unknown in countries where banks pay interest on checking accounts. Some of the other types of bank charges that are prevalent are:

- *Value dating.* This is a bank practice of taking value days as a form of compensation. *Forward-value dating* is when the receiving bank provides available funds on an incoming credit one or two business days forward. With *back-value dating,* the originating bank will back-value the debit to the account by one or two business days.

- *Turnover fees.* Some countries charge fees based on a percentage of the value of the *activity* (debit or credit) in the account.

- *Ad valorem.* Ad valorem charges are based on a percentage of the value of the *transaction,* for example, a percentage of the value of a wire transfer.

- *Fixed annual charge.* Some countries charge a fixed annual fee for access to the high-value payment system.

Appreciating and managing the complexities involved in each of the different countries in which a company is operating is analogous to playing three-dimensional chess. It requires attention at both the individual local level as well as at the overall corporate level. A regional focus can help to span that gap.

International Risk

One of the major differences in the job description of an international cash manager, compared with a domestic colleague, is the priority given to risk management. In the domestic environment, optimizing liquidity is *the* priority. Internationally, the impact of foreign exchange and other exposures is potentially far more significant than the saving of a few days of float or dollars on banking fees. Although there are risks arising in a domestic situation, such as interest rate and commodity risk, international business gives rise to many additional exposures.

Foreign Exchange Risk

Foreign exchange risk is a result of the fluctuation in the value of a foreign currency against the base, or home currency. A company doing business internationally can be exposed to any or all of the following types of risk:

- *Transaction exposure* results from a movement in foreign exchange rates between the time a transaction is booked and the time it settles, which can impact the overall value of the deal. For example, a deal entered into today, for payment in euro in 30 days, may be valued at $1 million at today's exchange rate. When the payment is due, however, the euro has weakened and at the prevailing exchange rates the amount received is now only $980,000.

- *Translation exposure* is the balance sheet exposure that results from a company's consolidating its financial statements on a global basis and reporting the change in the net value of its foreign currency assets. The exposure results from fluctuations in exchange rates from year to year, which changes the rate at which the net assets are valued.

- *Economic exposure* refers to the impact of fluctuating exchange rates on the value of future cash flows from long-term contracts. The longer the term of the contract, the greater the exposure.

Country Risk

Country risk, which refers to the specific risks of doing business in a foreign country, is comprised of several elements:

- *Political/sovereign risk* is the possibility that the actions of a sovereign government (e.g., nationalization or expropriation) or independent events (e.g., wars, riots, civil disturbances) may affect the ability of customers in that country to meet their obligations.

TIPS & TECHNIQUES

How to Obtain Better Foreign Exchange Rates

Cash managers should establish foreign exchange arrangements with at least two or three major banks, for several reasons:

- The rates that are quoted will reflect the bank's current position and appetite for a currency and the company's standing as a customer. Rates will vary from one bank to another even for the major currencies.

- Because deals settle at a future date, most banks require that a separate credit facility be put in place for foreign exchange. In order to ensure that a company has adequate credit in place to conduct its foreign exchange, arrangements may be required with more than one bank.

- Competitive pressure will improve the rates.

A better rate will be obtained if the bank is not informed whether the deal is to buy or sell a currency. Banks quote rates with a spread between the buying and selling rate. This is known as the *bid-offer spread* and represents the bank's profit margin. If the side of the market is undisclosed, the spread will be slimmer. Cash managers should also investigate the new online foreign exchange dealing products, such as FXall (*www.fxall.com*) and Currenex (*www.currenex.com*). These services will often provide a better rate than polling the banks by telephone.

- *Convertibility risk* refers to legal, regulatory, or logistical barriers that may prevent conversion of local currency into a foreign currency when a payment is due. This is particularly common in countries that have a shortage of hard currency at the central bank. In those situations, payments are queued, pending future availability of the currency.

- *Transfer risk,* caused by exchange control regulations, is the possibility that a borrower will be prohibited from transferring funds cross-border when the payment is due.

Cross-Border Commercial Risk

Cross-border commercial risk exists when goods move internationally. The specific risks are that:

- The exporter does not receive payment.

- The importer does not receive the goods expected, or the quality required, or in time.

In cross-border situations, these risks are exacerbated due to various factors:

- The difficulties of obtaining reliable credit information on trading partners

- The uncertainty of finding legal remedies in the event of a dispute

- The time for shipment and paperwork to arrive

- The need for instructions and value to pass through several banks in different countries to complete the transaction

The cash manager has to initially identify the specific risks to which the business is exposed, establish a system for measuring and monitoring exposures, and determine a strategy to manage the risk.

Eliminating Foreign Exchange Settlement Risk

Foreign exchange markets have traditionally settled on a "spot" basis, this is, two business days forward. This creates a risk between the trade date and settlement date, specifically called *Herstatt risk,* after the German bank that almost caused the collapse of the banking system in 1974, when its Luxembourg branch declared bankruptcy and failed to settle its foreign exchange contracts after receiving payment. In 2002 a new system called Continuous Link Settlement (CLS) was launched to eliminate the risk associated with cross-currency transactions. Approximately 40 banks can now settle foreign exchange transactions in the major currencies on a real-time basis (see Chapter 2).

Risk Management Tools

Hedging is the term used to define a company's actions to reduce or eliminate risk. The cost of hedging will depend on a number of variables, such as the instrument chosen, the amount being hedged, and the degree of risk being protected. Because hedging can be expensive, some companies choose to "self-insure" or to hedge only certain percentages and areas of their risk. These are perfectly legitimate strategies. The only indefensible strategy is to not hedge by default rather than as a result of a conscious decision.

A number of tools are available for managing risk. Many of the following vehicles can be used to hedge interest rate, foreign exchange, or commodity exposure.

Forward Contracts

A forward contract is an agreement between two parties to buy or sell a fixed amount of an asset at a rate established today for delivery on a specific date in the future. These arrangements can be customized as to amount and settlement date. Although markets can fluctuate both favorably and unfavorably, the predictability of a *certain* future cash flow is more important to a cash manager than taking the gamble on the direction of the markets. Forward contracts are used mainly to hedge transaction exposures. The fees are usually built into the price (i.e., the spread).

Futures Contracts

Although a futures contract is similar to a forward contract, in that it involves a fixed rate for purchase at a future date, futures differ in a number of other respects. The contracts are for large, standardized amounts and mature at fixed maturity dates. Futures are traded on securities exchanges and provide a great deal of flexibility, as they can be bought and sold at any time prior to maturity. In contrast, a forward contract is highly customized in terms of amount and maturity date and commits the cash manager to consummating the deal on settlement date.

Investors and speculators who want to take a position on the movement of the market over a period of time often use futures. Cash managers use them to hedge transaction or translation exposures. Futures are executed through a broker, who charges a commission.

Options

Options provide the right (but not the obligation) to buy or sell an asset at a specified price (the *strike price*) on or before a certain date. An American option allows the owner to exercise the option at any time prior to maturity. A European option can be exercised at maturity only. Options are traded through banks or brokers and are more expensive than forwards and futures, due to the lower volumes and lack of liquidity. In addition to a spread, brokers also charge a commission. Options do, however, provide considerable flexibility to the cash manager and are often used to hedge foreign exchange risk on fixed price contracts that have not yet been awarded.

Swaps

Swaps can be used for both risk and liquidity management. For a cash manager with a flow of foreign currency payables and ongoing currency exposure, a swap allows him or her to exchange (or swap) that set of cash flows against cash flows in domestic currency. These deals are established through brokers, and carry the risk that if the counterparty defaults, the cash manager reassumes the original obligation. Swaps are also used to exchange interest-rate or commodity floating-rate obligations for fixed-rate terms.

Another use of swaps is for liquidity management, where a company's temporary deficit in one currency can be covered by a surplus in another currency. The foreign exchange exposure is hedged by linking a spot transaction simultaneously to a forward transaction, converting back to the original currency. Swaps are usually executed at a "midrate" for the spot and forward, and are, therefore, cost advantageous over carrying out the two transactions independently, one on either side of the bid–offer spread.

Balance Sheet Matching

Translation exposure is measured as the change in value of the *net* amount of foreign currency assets (i.e., assets minus liabilities). One strategy for hedging this exposure is to offset foreign currency asset exposures with borrowings or liabilities in the same currency and country. Instead of funding a new plant overseas from the head office, a balance sheet hedge can be achieved by borrowing in the local currency and creating a same currency liability to offset the asset.

Leading and Lagging

Leading and lagging allows the cash manager to manipulate the timing of intercompany payables and receivables to take advantage of current foreign exchange rates or anticipated future movements.

- *Leading* refers to accelerating the timing of a transaction. If a receivable is in a currency that is depreciating, leading brings the transaction date forward to minimize the devaluation. A cash manager might also lead a payable in a currency that is appreciating, to minimize the cost of the transaction.

- *Lagging* is the delaying of the timing of a payment. If a receivable is in a currency that is strengthening, lagging delays the transaction date to maximize the appreciation. A cash manager might also lag a payable in a currency that is weakening to minimize the cost.

Leading and lagging are also used as liquidity management tools; for example, cash-rich subsidiaries can lead payments to subsidize the cash-poor divisions, or cash-poor units are allowed to lag their payments. However, this technique must be applied in a very controlled fashion to avoid the complications created by intercompany lending and the resulting withholding tax issues.

Letter of Credit

A letter of credit is a collection method that substitutes the credit risk of the importer with a bank assurance of payment upon performance by the exporter. The letter of credit specifies the precise terms of the contract. As long as the title and shipping documents presented by the exporter conform precisely to the requirements of the letter of credit, the bank issuing the letter of credit is obligated to pay the exporter, regardless of the status of the importer. For an additional fee, the exporter can choose to add the backing of a confirming bank to insure against the risk of default of the issuing bank. The confirming bank is usually located in the country of the exporter.

Due to the labor-intensive nature of the process and the credit risk being underwritten by the banking system, letters of credit are a relatively expensive service, although they provide the most protection to the exporter against nonpayment.

One of the most significant developments in recent years has been the digitization of the letter-of-credit process. A number of initiatives have undertaken to computerize all of the paper associated with a letter of credit, including the shipping documents, making them available on the Web. As a result, transmission, presentment, and discrepancy resolution are much more efficient. It is now not unusual for the paperwork to be concluded before the goods arrive.

Documentary Collections

Documentary collections assure an exporter that title to the goods being shipped will be delivered only against payment. This provides some protection to the exporter against nonpayment. The banking system, acting as agent for the exporter, retains custody of the title documents and delivers them to the buyer after he or she pays for the goods or commits to the payment. However, the exporter remains exposed to the risk of nonacceptance by the importer. Although retaining title, the goods are in a foreign country incurring storage costs while awaiting disposition. The options are to find another buyer, return the goods, or renegotiate the price, none of which are inexpensive options for the exporter.

Country Risk Insurance

Insuring against country risk can be difficult because the expected loss is normally not calculable. Unlike normal loss situations where loss history determines insurance rates, the probability of adverse government actions is more difficult to assess. Country risk insurance can sometimes be purchased from a company's own government, such as the Export Development Corporation (EDC) of Canada. This organization insures Canadian companies selling capital goods or services in foreign markets.

The principal organization offering country risk insurance is the Export-Import Bank (Ex-Im Bank), which protects exporters against the political and commercial risks of a foreign buyer defaulting on payment. Policies may be obtained for single or ongoing export sales. Various types of policies are available to accommodate the needs of exporters.

- *Short-term single and multibuyer.* The short-term single and multibuyer policy insures short-term sales with repayment terms of up to 180 days.

- *Medium-term single buyer.* Medium-term insurance is available for exporters of capital goods or services for terms up to five years.

- *Small business.* The Ex-Im Bank offers a short-term (up to 180 days) insurance policy geared to meet the credit requirements of smaller, less-experienced exporters.

Cross-Border Clearing and Settlement

The only certainty in cross-border clearing and settlement is that delays will be involved. The underlying cause of these delays is that all currencies must eventually settle in their country of origin. U.S. dollar checks will settle through the U.S. payment system. If the check is drawn in U.S. dollars on the account of a bank that is not a member of the U.S. payment system, the item must be returned to the drawee bank for collection. This manual process, involving numerous mail and processing delays, can take weeks.

Although the United Nations and the European Community (EC) are currently attempting to establish limited international guidelines,

IN THE REAL WORLD

Clearing Foreign Currency Items Offshore

There are a number of examples where a foreign currency (usually the U.S. dollar) is widely used in a local economy and arrangements have been made to *clear* locally drawn and payable items offshore. The U.K. Currency Clearing system clears checks drawn and payable in the City of London in U.S. dollars, Canadian dollars, Australian dollars, Japanese yen, and Swiss francs. Singapore offers U.S. dollar check clearing. Hong Kong, the Philippines, and Canada all clear electronic payments and checks in U.S. dollars. Ultimately, however, the currencies will *settle* across correspondent accounts in their country of domicile. U.S. dollars will settle in the United States; British pounds will settle in the United Kingdom.

cross-border movements of cash at present are not subject to any internationally accepted codes of performance, unlike trade transactions that are covered by International Chamber of Commerce (ICC) regulations.

Banks initiating wire transfers in foreign currencies will usually draw on the currency accounts (also called *nostro* accounts) established with their correspondent banks in the currency centers. If the correspondent bank has no direct relationship with the beneficiary bank, the instructions will pass through a chain of correspondent banks until a mutual relationship with the beneficiary bank is found. Even wire transfers can take five days or more before the credit is received. Specifying value dates and routing of the transfer to limit the number of correspondent banks involved in the process can speed up wire transfers.

TIPS & TECHNIQUES

Improving Cross–Border Collections

If business practice or cultural preferences dictate payment by check, a number of steps can be taken to improve cross-border collections:

- Request a check drawn on a bank that is a member of the currency clearing system.

- Have the items deposited directly to an account in the currency center.

- Collect closer to the customer. Several banks now offer international lockbox-type services (also called *intercept points*), described later in this chapter.

- Take advantage of local currency clearing where it is available.

- Use a cost-benefit analysis to determine when it becomes efficient to require electronic payments.

- Open an account at the same bank used by large customers, and have checks deposited directly to that account. This will ensure fast credit. Funds can be converted to the base currency and remitted to the concentration account as soon as they become available.

Basic International Cash Management Tools

Although companies have been managing their international cash flows for more than 20 years, it is only relatively recently that off-the-shelf cash management services have become widely available. Initially these products were offered only through the major global banks. However, smaller regional banks and third-party providers are now forming alliances and networks to offer international cash management services to their global customers. The growth of the Internet and improved communications technology means that many international services can now be offered without requiring physical branches worldwide. The principal tools are described in the sections that follow.

Electronic Banking Services

Many of the electronic services offered domestically are now available globally, although they are not necessarily identical to products offered in the U.S. Treasury workstations have long been able to automatically dial up banks' electronic reporting services, download the information, and insert the data into the company's spreadsheets. This process, known as *polling and parsing,* can now be done on a global scale to compile a consolidated balance report. Alternatively, a company can arrange for a cash management bank or third-party provider to consolidate and report the balances on its behalf.

Although global balance reporting is a well-established service, implementation and execution can still vary greatly by country and bank. A consolidated global balance report will be only as good as the weakest reporting location.

- Some banks (including branches of global banks) are not able to send transaction detail, only summary balances.

- Certain banks will send reports only when there has been activity, and so on some days there will be no report.

- Other banks may not have automated interfaces for balance reporting and may be keying information manually, which affects the accuracy and timeliness of the reporting.

- Real-time information is most readily available from banks doing business globally.

It is important that users' expectations be realistic as to what a global balance report can provide.

In the past, in order to be able to initiate transfers, a company had to subscribe to the proprietary electronic banking platforms of all their banks. These multiple subscriptions were not always convenient and posed additional access–security risks for the company. The SWIFT MT 101 message (see Appendix C) provides a solution by allowing a chosen "host" electronic banking platform to act as the conduit to transmit wire transfer messages to other banks.

The MT 101 is a message sent through an initial bank but destined for action by another financial institution. It can be used not only to pay funds but also to defund an account and consolidate balances with the concentration bank. Exhibit 7.2 illustrates how the MT 101 works, enabling a single electronic platform to manage an entire banking structure.

IN THE REAL WORLD

Bilateral Agreements

The MT 101 message type will prove to be very beneficial to treasurers. However, before it can be implemented, an agreement has to be in place between the customer and the "host" bank, and the host bank must also have executed a bilateral agreement (known as a *bilat*) with all the prospective recipient banks. The bilats are important because they define responsibilities and service levels between the parties. Some banks are even insisting on bilats with their own branches. Over the last few years, the major banks have been steadily increasing the number of bilats that are in place. A corporate customer with banking arrangements not covered by the existing agreements will have to wait until a new bilat is negotiated, which can require considerable time.

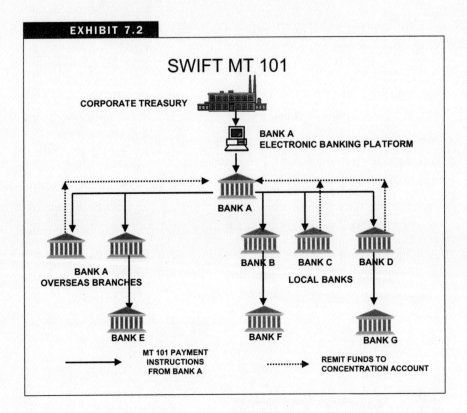

EXHIBIT 7.2

SWIFT MT 101

CORPORATE TREASURY

BANK A
ELECTRONIC BANKING PLATFORM

BANK A

BANK A
OVERSEAS BRANCHES

BANK B   BANK C   BANK D

LOCAL BANKS

BANK E   BANK F   BANK G

→ MT 101 PAYMENT
INSTRUCTIONS
FROM BANK A

┄┄┄► REMIT FUNDS TO
CONCENTRATION ACCOUNT

Foreign Currency Accounts

There are various options in establishing foreign currency accounts. The two major ones are:

1. *Centralized*. One of the simplest ways to manage foreign currency accounts is to maintain subaccounts in the branch of a single bank, often called a *multicurrency account*. Centralized currency accounts are easy to set up and maintain: there is one set of account-opening documentation, lower maintenance fees, and a single point of contact for customer service. The disadvantage is that a currency handled in a country other than that of its domicile is subject to availability delays upon deposit and up to two days delay on transfer. Cross-border currency transfers are usually done on a spot basis, that is, with two business days' notice.

2. *Decentralized.* The alternative way to maintain foreign currency accounts is to open accounts for each currency in its country of domicile. However, this may require opening up accounts with new banks; it can prove to be more labor-intensive to manage and monitor; and it may be more difficult to resolve customer service issues due to language and time zone differences. The advantages are that a currency in its own currency center will have better local deadlines, faster availability, and lower domestic pricing.

The decision whether to hold centralized or decentralized accounts will depend on the following:

- Volumes and amounts of individual currencies collected and disbursed

- The cash manager's ability to measure, monitor, and manage both currency exposure and multiple overseas banking relationships

- Sensitivity to administrative costs versus transaction costs

Each option carries trade-offs in terms of price, convenience, availability, and timing.

Most companies make a currency-by-currency decision as to whether to centralize or decentralize the location of the account, based on the nature, value, and volume of the flows. The resulting configuration will be a mix of both. Often, even though a currency might be held in a currency center account, there may also be an additional, second, centralized account for that currency as the top layer in a liquidity management structure.

International Lockboxes

The concept of a lockbox is valid anywhere in the world where payments are still being made by check, across a wide geographical area, and where there is a potential for mail, processing, and availability delays.

Although the precise mechanics may not be the same as in the United States, the effect of an international lockbox (also known as an *intercept point*) is to collect a check close to point of mailing, preferably in the same currency center, and to deposit the check into the local banking system as quickly as possible.

Collecting checks on a regional basis has value over transcontinental mailing and the subsequent collection process. Not only does an international lockbox reduce mail, processing, and availability float, it also minimizes transaction exposure by reducing the time it takes to collect a foreign currency. These services are beginning to be available in both Europe and Asia.

IN THE REAL WORLD

Collecting Foreign Currency Checks in the United States

A number of foreign currency checks still find their way into the hands of cash managers in the United States. The collection process can be long, and there are no international regulations on how quickly such items have to be handled. In addition to lost availability, the delay increases foreign exchange exposure.

Many banks offer to negotiate the check and provide immediate availability at a discount to the face value of the item, depending on the amount, the currency, and the importance of the corporate customer. The discount will reflect the bank's past experience on the length of time it takes to collect and will normally be on a recourse basis. Most importantly, however, the cash manager will have limited the transaction exposure.

Liquidity Management Tools

After risk management, liquidity management is one of the primary objectives of the international cash manager. Liquidity has to be addressed at both the local country level, as well as cross-border, in order to realize maximum efficiency of working capital. The following sections describe three of the major tools for managing international liquidity.

Notional Pooling

Notional pooling (also known as *interest allocation*) is a bank service that, on a daily basis, offsets debit and credit balances of a company's separate accounts to calculate a net balance. The bank pays interest on a positive overall position, or charges interest on a negative net balance. The individual balances never physically move and there is no commingling of funds. Notional pooling is available in most countries with a well-established, nationwide banking system.

The pooling calculation is performed entirely on the books of the bank. It can significantly cut the costs of borrowing for a company and improve returns on any cash surpluses. All balances have to be within the same bank network, which also contributes to rationalization of the banking structure. There is usually a requirement that the subsidiaries be reallocated debit or credit interest on an "arm's-length" basis, that is, at, or close to, market rates.

Notional pooling is a good tool for cash managers to administer intercompany liquidity. However, there are some issues with regard to pooling that vary by country. In some jurisdictions, only accounts of wholly-owned subsidiaries can be pooled. In others, resident and non-resident balances cannot be commingled, or pooling is prohibited entirely. Although the demand today from the corporate world is for cross-border, multicurrency notional pooling, tax and legal issues become considerably more complex, so this is not easily accomplished.

Cross-border Concentration

Cross-border concentration is used when notional pooling is not available or when the cash manager wants to consolidate the surplus positions in currency accounts. Because funds are concentrated into cash pools, there is often a confusion between notional pooling and concentration. Some banks use the terms interchangeably, especially when referring to cross-border pooling, when describing cross-border concentration into cash pools, rather than cross-border notional pooling.

Because cash concentration involves a physical movement of funds, often from a resident account to a nonresident concentration account, there are additional costs for the transfers, the possibility of availability delays, and increased administrative and reporting burdens.

Some banks offer an automated service by which they will draw down balances to a concentration account both for balances within their network and third-party banks. More often, however, the cash manager has to initiate the transfers manually, based on the balance reports and cash forecasts. The SWIFT MT 101 message type is becoming a valuable tool for effecting cross-border concentration.

Concentration is the technique most often used by companies that want to concentrate different currencies cross-border, as it allows maximum flexibility in managing liquidity. That said, concentration also entails a number of the tax and legal issues associated with intercompany lending, such as withholding taxes and thin capitalization.

Netting

Netting is a process that allows entities to offset total receivables against total payables. The concept has already been discussed in the context of clearing and settlement systems. Each entity either receives or pays a single net amount to the netting center in its local currency. Exhibit 7.3 illustrates the process.

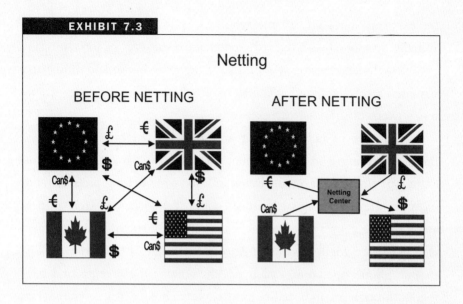

EXHIBIT 7.3

Netting

BEFORE NETTING

AFTER NETTING

- *Before netting.* Even if each subsidiary does only one trade with each of the others, there are a total of 12 transactions. Each subsidiary sells in its own currency, so there are four entities managing foreign exchange exposure and paying foreign exchange commissions on the total amount of the gross payables. The full value of the funds in transit results in a loss of availability of two to five days.

- *After netting.* Each subsidiary is involved in a single transaction in its own currency, either to receive from or pay to the netting center the net amount due. The transactions have been reduced to four, which represents a 67 percent offset ratio. Only one entity, the netting center, is involved in purchasing foreign exchange.

The most significant quantitative benefits result from the saving of foreign exchange commissions and the elimination of all collection float. Other benefits include reduction in treasury duplication, as the netting center can now act as the focus for cash flow, exposure, and reconciliation management. Treasury is also in a position to negotiate better exchange rates due to the wholesale amounts now being traded. Initially developed to reduce the costs and exposures of intracompany payables, modern netting systems increasingly accommodate third-party payables, receivables, and FX matching, which offset the foreign currency needs of subsidiaries.

A number of industries that are characterized by commoditized product offerings and large numbers of bilateral payments and receipts among participants have established industrywide netting programs. For example, the International Airlines Transport Association (IATA) operates a netting center between more than 200 airlines for both commercial and cargo flight payments. Another example is the world's GSM mobile phone operators, which net their incoming receipts and payments through an industry-netting center. These netting systems can produce over 80 percent offset ratios, resulting in significant cost savings to the industry.

Netting systems are relatively easy to establish, requiring only a computer program within a treasury center. However, their success depends on the involvement of all the parties. Many companies are putting such applications on their intranet or the Web for input. This provides direct access to the software, prompt resolution of discrepancies, and faster notification of changes to all participants. Using a Web-based system also puts the cost of netting within the reach of smaller companies. As with pooling, some countries impose restrictions on the use of netting or require prior central bank approval.

Treasury Structures

There are various models for structuring treasury to manage international flows. The trend is toward greater centralization on a regional basis to realize economies of scale and reduce duplication of systems, people, and functions.

Tax-advantaged Centers

A number of countries offer tax incentives and other benefits to attract multinational businesses to manage their treasury and other shared functions through a local subsidiary. Attracting international business into the country provides revenue and employment. Some of the major vehicles include the International Financial Services Company (IFSC) in Ireland, the Belgian Coordination Center (BCC), Swiss and Luxembourg Holding Companies, and Singapore's Operational Headquarters (OHQ).

Reinvoicing Centers

Reinvoicing centers are used by the larger multinational companies to centralize all intracompany buying and selling. Subsidiaries no longer deal directly with each other, but place their orders through the reinvoicing center. Although title passes to the center, the goods continue to be shipped directly to the purchasing subsidiary. The center gives the company more control over international flows, while providing both quantitative and qualitative benefits, including centralization of foreign exchange exposure and improved worldwide liquidity management.

IN THE REAL WORLD

Pressure on Tax-advantaged Centers

It should be noted that centers within the Economic and Monetary Union (EMU) are under considerable pressure to phase out the benefits of these vehicles in favor of greater standardization and harmonization of tax regimes within the union. In the future, companies seeking the benefits of a tax-advantaged vehicle from which to manage their treasury may be forced to consider locations outside the EMU.

However, along with pooling and netting, reinvoicing centers are often highly regulated and frequently under scrutiny by local tax authorities for demonstrable arm's-length pricing.

In-house Banks (IHB)

Many larger companies establish an in-house bank to coordinate and centralize all the banking activities on behalf of their subsidiaries. In addition to being a source of global funding, the in-house bank also provides foreign currency accounts, investment, liquidity management, and netting and pooling services.

Commissionaire Structure

Certain industries, such as software developers, lend themselves to the commissionaire structure, especially those with one or two regional manufacturing plants that supply a number of subsidiaries. The commissionaire principal, usually located in a tax-friendly country, undertakes all required interfaces with the manufacturing facility, vendors, and suppliers. The subsidiaries act as sales agents for the principal, earning a commission on sales. This allows for:

- Concentration of profits in the country of the principal
- Centralization of foreign exchange exposure
- More effective liquidity management
- Circumvention of many of the intercompany lending issues that arise when cash accumulates in subsidiary accounts, as the cash flows belong to and are under the control of the principal

European Developments

In 1999, 11 European Community (EC) countries took the unprecedented step of uniting their economies and currency, forming the Economic and Monetary Union (EMU). Greece joined the EMU in 2001. The European Central Bank (ECB) was established to oversee monetary policy for the EMU. The euro is now the single currency of the EMU. Three EC countries, Sweden, Denmark, and the United Kingdom, decided to defer the decision to join the EMU to some future, unspecified date.

To assist the ECB in managing and implementing monetary policy, the Trans-European Automated Real-Time Gross Settlement Express Transfer System (TARGET) was developed. The RTGS systems of the national central banks link to TARGET to effect euro transfers cross-border in real time. TARGET is a communications system, not a money transfer system, and settlement occurs across the interlinking accounts at the national central banks. Access to TARGET is not limited to the central banks of the EMU. Any central bank that has an RTGS system that clears euro can be linked, albeit on slightly restricted terms. As a result, the national central banks of Sweden, Denmark, and the United Kingdom all have real-time links to TARGET. For cash managers, the introduction of TARGET means that for the first time funds can move cross-border, between banks, intraday.

The Impact of the Euro

The introduction of the euro has had significant implications for cash managers:

- As all EMU countries have the same currency, there is no intra-EMU foreign exchange exposure to be managed.

- FX commissions and transfer costs have been considerably reduced.

- Managing EMU-wide euro liquidity has now become the primary focus.

- Banking relationships are being consolidated. Although there may still be legitimate reasons for retaining some local accounts, such as for more efficient collections or maintaining vendor relationships, there are significant opportunities for rationalizing the banking structure within the euro zone.

With the emphasis turning from FX exposure management to liquidity management, companies have been greatly assisted by the new clearing systems that allow same-day cross-border transfers. Prior to TARGET, the only way to accomplish a same-day transfer was through the branches of a global bank.

New Euro Payment Systems

While TARGET remains the principal vehicle for the central banks to manage liquidity, and for urgent high-value cross-border payments, other less-expensive payment systems have been established (or are in development) for the corporate world.

- The Euro Banking Association (EBA) operates a high-value net settlement system for members called EURO1 that clears through TARGET at the end of the day and settles through a settlement account at the European Central Bank.

- RTGS^{plus} provides real-time gross settlement (through the RTGS^{plus} settlement account at the Deutsche Bundesbank) for interbank and customer payments.

- The EBA's STEP1 offers a low-value euro payment system.

- A number of initiatives are under way to provide pan-European batch payments through ACH-like systems, such as the EBA's STEP2.

The changes in Europe have provided cash managers with an opportunity to reengineer their European banking structure and make EMU-wide liquidity management much more efficient.

Tips for Emerging Global Treasurers

For a company not accustomed to the intricacies of managing the cash flows of a global business, the following guidelines and tips can be helpful when putting together an international cash management system.

Basic Tips

- *Set realistic expectations about what can be achieved.* Be prepared for things to be very different across the border. Do not take at face value services that purport to be "global." It will not be possible to completely replicate the level of U.S. service.

- *Stay open-minded.* Do not underestimate the value of local knowledge. It is possible that local solutions and systems may be more advanced or more appropriate in local conditions. For example, Scandinavia has been using sophisticated Wireless Applications Protocol (WAP) technology for a number of years. Giro systems (that often operate through local post offices) can be much more cost-effective than using bank services for low-value domestic payments.

- *Be sure you need what you ask for.* Will the product or service be truly useful and worth the price paid? There is a point at which real-time information becomes irrelevant in a different time zone.

- *Keep options broad.* When selecting service providers, there are more choices today than ever before. A few "global" banks have dominated the market for many years. Recent innovations mean that through technology and judicious alliances, smaller regional banks, ASPs, and other nonbank providers can now offer many international services cost effectively.

- Seek the professional advice of a banker, tax expert, accountant, or consultant.

Intermediate Tips

- *Take it in stages.* Work from the local level first. Start by making cash management as efficient as possible in the local environment before tackling regional efficiencies.

- *Realize that managing liquidity on a global scale may not be optimal.* Most companies find that managing on a regional basis provides the most efficient solution.

- *Review banking structures, services, and costs often and carefully.* Companies may be reluctant to institute change unless momentous events have occurred, especially as implementations are frequently painful. But as the company or the environment changes, cash management needs should be reviewed.

- *Reexamine European banking arrangements in light of the opportunities afforded by the EMU and euro.* Centralize functions, consolidate banks, and manage eurowide liquidity.

- *Negotiate pricing for all euro transfers, both local and cross-border.* Many companies are insisting that all euro transfers be priced at domestic or near-domestic levels.

- *Expand the use of procurement cards to international retail payments.* Cross-border, low-value payments can be particularly expensive. Using procurement cards for these disbursements can realize significant savings and efficiencies.

Advanced Tips

- *Use direct debits wherever possible.* In many countries, direct debits are used as a routine and efficient domestic collection mechanism. This mechanism can also be used for cross-border collections.

- *Recognize that international ACH is coming.* A number of proprietary services already link the U.S.'s domestic ACH with similar systems overseas. However, the latest initiatives will offer open access to cross-border, low-value mass payment systems.

- *Outsource noncore functions.* International business is complex and requires high levels of expertise, knowledge, and investment in systems and technology. The costs can be high if borne internally.

- *Put shared cash management functions on the Web.* Balance reporting, bill paying, transfers, letters of credit, and netting are all standard ASP applications available over the Internet.

- *Get rid of the paper.* Take advantage of the new services that offer electronic letters of credit and documentary collections.

- *Be tax-aware, not tax-foolish.* Tax rules and regulations are complex, varied, and subject to change without notice. Minimizing taxes paid on a worldwide basis is a worthy goal, but not the only goal.

In conclusion, ask questions, lots of them. Many companies have faced the same issues. Banks are a logical first contact for more information. Local treasury associations or user groups are a good source of knowledge. The Internet can also provide access to the experience of companies that would normally be difficult to reach. The AFP's *Standardized RFPs for Global Treasury Services* (see Chapter 9 for a summary of contents) is an excellent starting point when preparing an RFP for international services.

Summary

This chapter examined the complexities of doing business internationally. When a company first starts to "go global," it is not unusual that cash management is not a high priority. The numbers are too small; and most often, global subsidiaries are allowed to retain their autonomy and carry on very much as before. However, as international flows grow to be significant, it becomes important to rationalize the banking structure and manage the risk and liquidity more efficiently.

CASE STUDY

As a first step, Rick Shaw will have to do a lot of information gathering before making any changes. Risks have to be assessed, objectives set, and tools evaluated. It is certain that there will be opportunities for managing the liquidity in Europe more efficiently. It is very likely that some of these initiatives will be applicable in other areas of the globe as well. At the very least, Rick will be reassessing current banking relationships, services, and prices.

CHAPTER 8

United States Banking Environment

After reading this chapter, you will be able to

- Understand the U.S. banking system
- Appreciate the role of the Federal Reserve
- Review the important legislation and the impact of deregulation
- Evaluate the account analysis statement
- Consider some practical ideas for improving a company's use of cash management services
- Understand UCC rules pertaining to banking services

CASE STUDY

Bill Fold, the treasurer of GETDOE, has been asked to explain the U.S. banking environment to his colleagues from Europe. Now that the overseas divisions are being integrated into the U.S. company, and treasury is being centralized, it is important that the new businesses understand the context of the home office. Ann I. Shade, Bill's cash manager, has been recruited to assist in preparing a document to explain how the banking system is structured, the major legislation and regulations affecting cash management, and the impact of deregulation on the industry.

T he complex nature of the U.S. banking structure and the vast geo-graphical territory covered give rise to the need for sophisticated cash management techniques. The large number of depository insti-tutions and intricate interbank payment networks required to handle the volume and rapid turnover has shaped the payment system. To ensure that these function efficiently and reliably, the Federal Reserve plays an important role in regulating and operating the payment systems, in addi-tion to providing payment services to financial institutions. The legisla-tion that has been enacted over the years has also greatly influenced how the industry has evolved and the types of services the banks have devel-oped to assist corporate treasuries manage their cash flows.

The Role and Services of Financial Institutions

Although the number is constantly changing, there are in excess of 18,000 financial institutions in the United States. These are comprised of commercial banks and thrift institutions, including credit unions, sav-ings and loan associations, federal savings banks, and mutual savings banks.

Depository institutions play a central role in the payment system, with the vast majority of payments originating from demand deposit, or checking accounts. Since the early 1980s, all depository institutions have access to the Federal Reserve payment systems. Commercial banks offer a wide range of services (see Exhibit 8.1), while thrift institutions play a more limited role, accepting consumer deposits and lending money, primarily for home mortgage loans.

Regulation of the Banking Industry

Traditionally, depository institutions performed an intermediation func-tion, acting as a link between those with funds to invest and those with a need to borrow. Much of the legislation in the 1900s was enacted to protect that role and prevent conflicts of interest. It was only toward the

EXHIBIT 8.1

Commercial Bank Services

Checking Accounts	There are two types of checking account: the demand deposit account (DDA), which traditionally does not pay interest; and the hybrid account that combines the features of a demand and savings account, such as the negotiable order of withdrawal (NOW) and money market deposit accounts.
Credit Services	Short- and long-term credit facilities, as well as a range of special-purpose loans, such as mortgages.
Payment and Collection Services	Clearing checks and effecting electronic transfers.
Investment Services	A wide range of investments from the overnight sweep accounts to mutual funds and long-term time deposits and certificates of deposit.
Risk Management Services	Swaps, options, forwards, futures, and other derivatives to reduce or eliminate a customer's exposure to foreign exchange, interest rate, or commodity price risk.
Investment Banking Services	Services associated with issuing commercial paper, the sale of loans, and private placements, and consulting services on mergers and acquisitions and corporate structure.
Trade Services	Services to assist in the financing and collection of trade obligations, such as letters of credit, documentary collections, and bankers' acceptances (BAs).
Agent and Fiduciary Services	Managing assets whose title remains with the owner. Examples of these services are: registrar, transfer agent, paying agent, custody services, corporate pension plans, qualified employee benefit plans, and corporate trustee.

end of the century that deregulation began to free up the industry and, as a result, change the structure and nature of banks and banking in the United States.

Functions of the Federal Reserve System

The Banking Panic of 1907 proved to be the most severe of four in the previous 34 years. The banking system was prone to bank failures and the U.S. dollar was not responsive to changes in demand. Major bank reform was needed but it took until 1913 before the Federal Reserve Act established a central bank for the United States. Acting as an independent agency of the U.S. government, the Federal Reserve (the Fed) undertook five principal roles:

1. Conduct the nation's monetary policy, by expanding and contracting the money supply through open market activities involving the buying and selling of U.S. government securities.

2. Supervise and regulate banking institutions and protect the credit rights of consumers. The Fed has jurisdiction over all bank holding companies, all state member banks, their nonbank subsidiaries, their foreign subsidiaries, and *Edge Act* banks (corporations through which banks conduct nondomestic business).

3. Maintain the stability of the financial system by assuring the smooth functioning and continued development of the nation's payment system. The Fed plays a key role in the following:

   - *Fedwire.* The Fed operates the domestic real-time gross settlement electronic transfer system.

   - *Automated Clearing House (ACH) system.* The Fed is the principal operator of the ACH net settlement system, which processes and clears low-value batch payments.

   - *Check clearing.* The Fed clears checks through its network back to the drawee bank.

4. Provide certain financial services to the U.S. government. The Fed acts as fiscal agent for the U.S. treasury by maintaining checking accounts at the Reserve banks, paying bills, collecting taxes,

and making transfers such as paying Social Security benefits. The Reserve banks also handle the operations involved in selling, servicing, and redeeming marketable treasury securities.

5. Develop and administer regulations that implement major federal laws.

When the Fed was originally established in 1913, the primary vehicle for central bank operations was expected to be lending reserve funds through the discount window. Today, open market operations have superceded the discount window as the principal instrument for implementing monetary policy. The discount window still plays an important secondary role by extending credit to relieve liquidity strains in the banking system, acting as a safety valve by alleviating pressure in reserve markets.

Organization of the Fed

The Fed is organized into three main divisions:

1. *Board of Governors.* The Board's primary function is the formulation of monetary policy. In addition, the Board has broad supervisory and regulatory responsibilities over the activities of banks that are members of the payment system. Seven members serve a 14-year term. Appointment to the Board is by the President of the United States.

2. *Federal Open Market Committee (FOMC).* The FOMC implements the Federal Reserve's national monetary policy by making key decisions regarding the conduct of open market operations. Through buying and selling of U.S. government and other securities, the FOMC can inject or absorb liquidity into the market. In addition to the seven Board members, the FOMC consists of five Reserve bank presidents, one of whom is the president of the Federal Reserve Bank of New York. The other four members serve on a rotating basis.

3. *Federal Reserve District Banks.* The Fed conducts business through a nationwide network of 12 Federal Reserve Banks (see Exhibit 8.2 for a map of the Federal Reserve Bank Districts).

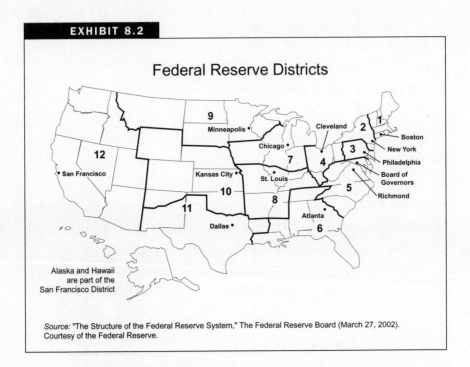

EXHIBIT 8.2

Federal Reserve Districts

9
Minneapolis
Cleveland 2 1
Boston
Chicago
New York
12
7
3
Philadelphia
San Francisco
Kansas City
4
Board of
St. Louis
Governors
10
5
11
8
Richmond
Atlanta
Dallas
6

Alaska and Hawaii
are part of the
San Francisco District

Source: "The Structure of the Federal Reserve System," The Federal Reserve Board (March 27, 2002). Courtesy of the Federal Reserve.

The services provided to depository institutions are similar to those provided by banks to business customers. The district banks hold the cash reserves and make loans. They move currency and coin into and out of circulation and collect and process 17 billion checks a year. In addition to the 12 Reserve banks, there are 25 branches of these banks and regional check processing centers (RCPCs) around the country to facilitate check clearing.

Other Regulatory Agencies

A number of other agencies share the responsibility for supervising banks with the Fed. These are:

- *Office of the Comptroller of the Currency (OCC).* The OCC grants charters to national banks and is directly responsible for their regulation and supervision.

- *Federal Deposit Insurance Corporation (FDIC).* The FDIC directly supervises FDIC-insured state-chartered banks and commercial banks that are not members of the Fed. The FDIC provides insurance on deposits of up to $100,000 per personal or corporate account per insured institution. The FDIC is also usually appointed as the receiver in the case of a bank failure and is tasked with liquidating the bank's assets, paying insured depositors, or finding an acquirer.

- *Securities and Exchange Commission (SEC).* The securities market is regulated and supervised by the SEC, which establishes the procedures and disclosure requirements for companies that sell their securities to the public. The SEC is the registering agent for public offerings of debt and securities and is also responsible for regulating investment advisors and mutual funds.

- *Department of Justice (DOJ).* The Department of Justice plays a role in reviewing the impact of proposed bank mergers and acquisitions under the various antitrust laws, including the Sherman and Clayton Acts. Although originally instituted to protect consumers from monopolies and oligopolies, the antitrust laws have broadened in scope to include all areas of business, including banks.

Dual Banking System

The United States has a dual banking system that allows commercial banks to elect to be federally or state-chartered. The major difference

IN THE REAL WORLD

National versus State-Chartered Banks

Today, the difference between banks that are nationally or state-chartered is minimal, as over 95 percent of all commercial banks are members of and, therefore, subject to supervision by the FDIC. Furthermore, *all* depository institutions are subject to oversight and reserve requirements imposed by the Fed.

used to be one of supervision and regulation. All banks, federal or state-chartered, that are members of the Fed must also be insured by the FDIC and, therefore, will be regulated by a combination of the Board of Governors of the Fed, the OCC, and the FDIC. Federally chartered banks must belong to the Federal Reserve System. State-chartered banks that are not members of the Federal Reserve System, on the other hand, are supervised by the state banking boards and commissions.

Significant Legislation

Historically, legislation was introduced to resolve contemporary crises in the banking environment. With the passage of time, however, some acts have become less relevant in the current world. The following is a review of the major legislation that affects today's banking industry and the impact of deregulation on cash management. Exhibit 8.3 (see the end of this section) summarizes the legislation that has been important in shaping the U.S. banking environment.

Regulation of the Industry

Several laws were introduced to regulate the industry, usually in response to failures of the banking system. Some of the most important that are responsible for determining today's banking environment are described in the following subsections.

Federal Reserve Act of 1913. The *1864 National Bank Act* was the first to attempt to regulate the industry by establishing a national banking system and the chartering of national banks. Unfortunately, widespread bank failures and panics continued until Congress adopted the Federal Reserve Act in 1913. The 1913 Act established the Federal Reserve System as the central bank of the United States. The purpose of the Fed was to provide a stable currency and to improve supervision of banking.

The Securities Laws of 1933, 1934 and 1940. In the wake of the Great Depression and recognition of the need to bring supervision and regulation to the securities industry, these laws established the Securities and Exchange Commission (SEC), with powers to oversee and govern the issuance of securities.

Leveling the Playing Field

For many years, foreign banks operating in the United States were not subject to the same controls and regulations as domestic banks. Several laws have been introduced both to subject foreign banks to U.S. regulatory supervision and to provide U.S. banks with a more equal competitive footing. The most important act for cash managers is the Edge Act.

Edge Act of 1919. After the First World War, Americans came home with a different view of the world and an interest in developing business internationally. The Edge Act permitted banks to conduct international business across state lines as a means of enabling them to better compete with foreign banks that were not restricted by state boundaries. One of the newest Edge Act banks is CLS Bank, Inc., established in 2002 to process the foreign exchange transactions for the new Continuous Link Settlement (CLS) process. CLS was developed to remove the risk inherent in delayed settlement in the foreign exchange markets (see Chapter 7).

Deregulation

Deregulation of the banking industry has been ongoing for the last 20 years, although the legacy of prior legislation continues to influence the current-day environment. The following are some of the most significant acts that have attempted to dismantle legislation that has become outdated.

Depository Institutions Deregulation and Monetary Control Act of 1980 (DIDMCA). The era of deregulation during the Reagan Administration led to many sweeping and significant changes, as implemented by the DIDMCA, principally:

- To allow banks to compete more effectively with thrift institutions for funds, *negotiable orders of withdrawal* (NOW) accounts were created. NOW accounts are checking accounts that pay interest on balances and are available to individuals, governments, and not-for-profit organizations.

- Interest rate ceilings on deposits imposed by Regulation Q were phased out for all except corporate accounts.

- The Depository Institutions Deregulation Committee was established to prescribe rules governing the payment of interest and dividends and the establishment of classes of deposits or accounts.

- All deposit institutions were required to maintain reserves at the Fed, and the deposit insurance ceiling was raised to $100,000.

- In return for maintaining reserves, all depository institutions were allowed access to Fed services, such as the discount window and check clearing.

- Previously free Fed services were priced at market rates.

- The Fed was mandated to take steps to either reduce or price payment system float. This had a significant impact on the disbursement services offered by banks.

Riegle-Neal Interstate Banking and Branching Efficiency Act of 1994 (IBBEA). The McFadden Act was introduced in 1927 in an attempt to protect state banking business by prohibiting branching and accepting deposits across state lines. This effectively established the state boundary as the primary limit for bank expansion and allowed the states to decide the extent of branching within and outside state borders. The act was amended by the Douglas Amendment (also known as the Bank Holding Company Act) in 1956, which allowed banks to merge across state lines if jointly approved by the individual states. In 1994, the IBBEA took deregulation the final step and permitted banks, effective June 1997, to merge across state lines, provided they were adequately capitalized and managed.

Impact of IBBEA. The IBBEA is expected to restructure the nation's banking industry. The large multistate bank holding companies that are currently being formed are increasingly concentrating the volume of payments being processed through fewer channels. This gives the banks opportunities to achieve economies of scale and technological efficiencies in their back offices.

Nationwide branching provides significant cash management benefits to companies in terms of efficiencies in collection, concentration, and disbursements. Using a bank with countrywide branches means that cash flows will no longer have to be managed through complex collection and concentration structures; and the mail float associated with disbursements will disappear because all deposits and disbursements will be treated as local items. Efficient interstate banking may be one of the major motivators in moving the payments industry toward greater use of electronic payments.

It seems unlikely, however, that the United States will have a true nationwide retail banking system in the near term. This is partially due to the extreme fragmentation of the banking industry. Those few banks with a coast-to-coast presence (albeit limited in terms of branching) have also had to deal with massive conversions of legacy systems to uniform platforms.

The mergers of the last decade have either been to consolidate existing regional strength, such as Wells Fargo/First Interstate/Norwest and Fleet/Bank of Boston, or to complement core competencies, such as Deutsche Bank/Bankers Trust and J. P. Morgan/Chase. Even though expansion of territory has been achieved in some of the more recent

Cash Management and Interstate Banking

The advent of interstate banking will present treasury managers with many cash management benefits. The total number of banks can be reduced and integrated, and uniform banking platforms will provide more efficient collections, concentration, and disbursement of funds. It is possible to envisage that pooling opportunities (see Chapter 7) will be available in the future. Today, companies with an extensive regional business may already benefit by consolidating their business with one of the super-regional banks that has extensive retail and commercial presence in a number of contiguous states.

mergers, and several banks now have a significant retail presence in multiple states, such as Wells Fargo, Bank One, Wachovia, and Bank of America, no one bank can claim to be truly nationwide.

Gramm–Leach–Bliley Act (GLB) of 1999. The Glass–Steagall Act of 1933 (also known as the Banking Act of 1933) was another measure introduced to protect the economy from future market crashes by separating commercial banking from investment banking and eliminating conflicts of interest. The act shaped the development of the banking industry and the structure of financial institutions for the next 60 years, until fully repealed in 1999 by GLB. The 1999 Act creates a new financial holding company; and while there are certain restrictions on the nonfinancial activities in which the new company can engage, they are authorized to:

- Engage in underwriting and selling insurance and securities
- Conduct both commercial and merchant banking

- Invest in and develop real estate and other "complementary activities"

GLB also allows national banks to underwrite municipal bonds, and introduces significant consumer protection provisions, preventing the unauthorized disclosure of nonpublic information to unaffiliated third parties.

Customer Rights

As part of its role in supervising and regulating the industry, the Fed has always been concerned with defining and protecting consumers' rights. Following are some of the most significant acts that have impacted business banking.

Electronic Funds Transfer Act of 1978 (EFTA). Rapid developments in technology and the increased use of electronic services such as ACH and ATMs led to congressional mandates regarding usage. This act defines the rights and responsibilities of individuals with respect to electronic funds transfers (including debit cards), with the exception of wire transfers. It covers direct deposits such as payroll, Social Security benefits, and preauthorized payments, for example, automatic payment of utility bills. Individuals have the right to stop a preauthorized payment as long as the financial institution is given three days notice. The liability on cards is limited as long as the card is reported lost or stolen.

An amendment in 1996, the electronic funds transfer (EFT) provision of the Debt Collection Improvement Act, required that most federal payments, with the exception of tax refunds, be made by EFT in lieu of paper checks. This resulted in banks developing electronic services for payment of corporate taxes; and NACHA launched the TXP message type specifically for ACH tax payments (see Appendix B).

EXHIBIT 8.3

Chronology of Major Banking Legislation

Federal Reserve Act of 1913	Established the Federal Reserve System, creating a central bank for the United States.
Edge Act of 1919	Permitted banks to conduct international business across state lines.
McFadden Act 1927	Prohibited branching and accepting deposits across state lines.
Glass-Steagall Act of 1933 (Banking Act of 1933)	Separated commercial banking from investment banking and established them as separate lines of business. It created the FDIC as a temporary agency to guarantee deposits. The act put in place interest-rate ceilings and prohibited the payment of interest on demand accounts.
Securities Laws of 1933, 1934 and 1940	Established the Securities and Exchange Commission (SEC) to supervise and regulate the securities industry.
Banking Act of 1935	Established the FDIC as a permanent agency of the government.
Douglas Amendment of 1956	Allowed banks to merge across state lines if jointly approved by individual states.
International Banking Act of 1978	Brought foreign banks within the federal regulatory framework. It required deposit insurance for branches of foreign banks engaged in retail deposit taking in the United States.
Electronic Funds Transfer Act of 1978 (EFTA)	Established the roles and responsibilities of the parties involved in electronic funds transfers (except wire transfers). Also limited consumer liability for fradulent transactions at ATMs and POS terminals.
Financial Institutions Regulatory and Interest Rate Control Act of 1978 (FIRIRCA)	Created the Federal Financial Institutions Examination Council, to promote uniform supervisory and examination policies for federally insured depository institutions, including a uniform system for rating banks. It also established limits and reporting requirements for bank insider transactions.

EXHIBIT 8.3 CONTINUED

Depository Insitutions Deregulation and Monetary Control Act of 1980 (DIDMCA)	Established NOW accounts; abolished interest rate ceilings for all but corporate demand accounts; raised FDIC insurance to $100,000; required all depository institutions to maintain reserves; allowed all depository institutions access to Fed services; priced Fed services at market rates; mandated a reduction in payment system float.
Garn-St. Germain Act of 1982 (Depository Institutions Act)	Expanded the powers of the FDIC to assist troubled banks. It established the Net Worth Certificate Program and extended the powers of thrift institutions. In response to the flood of bank failures in the early 1980s, it also began to chip away at the McFadden Act by allowing the FDIC to arrange cross-state bank mergers if suitable in-state partners could not be found.
Competitive Equality Banking Act of 1987 (CEBA)	Formally legitimized the rights of existing nonbank banks such as Sears, Roebuck & Co, and American Express, which were now able to operate limited-service banks in direct competition with commercial banks.
Expedited Funds Availability Act of 1988	Defined procedures and timing for returning checks and the maximum periods before deposited checks become available for withdrawal.
Financial Institutions Reform, Recovery and Enforcement Act of 1989 (FIRREA)	Restored the public's confidence in the savings and loan industry. It gave the FDIC the responsibility for insuring the deposits of thrift institutions. FIRREA expanded prohibitions against insider activities and created new Truth in Savings provisions and gave the FDIC increased flexibility in raising the insurance premiums it charged to banks and thrifts.

EXHIBIT 8.3 CONTINUED

Federal Deposit Insurance Corporation Improvement Act (FDICIA) of 1991	Amended FIRREA by mandating a least-cost resolution method and a prompt action approach to the problem of failing banks and ordered the creation of a risk-based insurance assessment. It established higher standards for financial institution safety and required the FDIC to declare insolvent any bank or thrift that failed to maintain equity capital to 2 percent of its assets.
Riegle-Neal Interstate Banking and Branching Efficiency Act of 1994 (IBBEA)	Effective 1997, permitted banks to acquire banks and merge across state lines in states that passed legislation permitting branching, provided they were adequately capitalized.
Gramm-Leach Bliley Act of 1999 (GLB)	Established the creation of new financial holding companies that are allowed to engage in underwriting, selling insurance and securities, commercial and merchant banking, developing real estate, and other "complementary activities."
Electronic Signatures in Global and National Commerce Act of 2000	Established the legality of electronic or digital signatures in e-commerce transactions.

Source: www.federalreserve.org, "The Structure of the Federal Reserve System," March 27, 2002.

The provisions of this act are incorporated in Federal Reserve Regulation E, which was revised in 2001 to require the disclosure of certain fees associated with automated teller machine (ATM) transactions. It was further revised in 2002 to cover electronic check conversion and authorization of recurring debits.

Expedited Funds Availability Act 1988 (EFAA). In an attempt to curb some of the abuses that were occurring in the banking industry, Congress passed EFAA to reduce the time a financial institution can hold a check before making the funds available to a depositor. The

EFAA established new standards for expedited funds availability, as well as return procedures for payable through drafts and checks. The provisions of this act are incorporated into Regulation CC.

Electronic Signatures in Global and National Commerce Act 2000. Recognizing the growing use of the Internet, e-commerce, and cross-border transactions, this act gave digital signatures the same authority as ink signatures. The act also provided for the enforceability of electronic transactions.

Federal Reserve Regulations Impacting Cash Managers

The payments system in the United States is governed by a patchwork of federal and state laws, Federal Reserve Regulations, and case law. Federal Reserve Regulations are used by the Board of Governors to implement the laws pertaining to banking and financial activities. Exhibit 8.4 summarizes the regulations that most impact cash managers.

The Account Analysis

Regulation Q (included in Exhibit 8.4) prohibits the payment of interest on corporate DDAs. In understanding the impact of this regulation on bank billing practices, it is necessary to review the standard invoice used by commercial banks—the account analysis. The term is derived from the evaluation of the account for the purpose of determining the account's surplus or deficit position when consideration is given to two categories of activities:

- The account's balances
- Cash management service charges

Although interest cannot be paid on the corporate DDA, banks will allow an "earnings credit" to be offset against service charges based on the level of balances in the account.

EXHIBIT 8.4

Summary of Federal Reserve Regulations

Regulation	Title
A	*Extensions of Credit by Federal Reserve Banks.* Governs borrowing by depository institutions at the Federal Reserve window. Subsequent amendments address changes in the basic discount rate.
B	*Equal Credit Opportunity.* Prohibits lenders from discriminating against credit applicants. It establishes guidelines for gathering and evaluating credit information and requires written notification when credit is denied.
D	*Reserve Requirements of Depository Institutions.* Sets uniform requirements for all depository institutions to maintain reserve balances either with their Federal Reserve Bank or as cash in their vaults. By setting different levels of reserves for different types of deposit, the Fed can use this mechanism to control the supply of money.
E	*Electronic Funds Transfers.* Establishes the rights, liabilities, and responsibilities of parties in electronic funds transfers (EFT) and protects consumers when they use such systems. In 2001, an amendment became effective that requires banks to disclose fees for using automated teller machines. In 2002, revisions addressing electronic check-conversion transactions and electronic authorization of recurring debits became mandatory.
J	*Collection of Checks and Other Items by Federal Reserve Banks and Funds Transfers through Fedwire.* Establishes procedures, duties, and responsibilities among: a) Federal Reserve Banks, b) the senders and payors of checks and certain other items, and C) the senders and recipients of wire transfers.
K	*International Banking Operations.* Governs the international banking operations of U.S. banking organizations and the operations of foreign banks in the United States.

EXHIBIT 8.4 CONTINUED

Regulation	Title
M	*Consumer Leasing.* Implements the consumer leasing provisions of the Truth in Lending Act by requiring meaningful disclosure of leasing terms.
P	*Privacy of Consumer Financial Information.* Implements the provisions of the Gramm-Leach-Bliley Act that prohibits a financial institution from disclosing nonpublic personal information to third parties that are not affiliated with the financial institution.
Q	*Prohibition against Payment of Interest on Demand Deposits.* Prohibits member banks from paying interest on demand deposits. The DIDMCA lifted this restriction in 1986 from all parties except corporations. It is expected that the remaining provisions will be phased out in the near future.
Y	*Bank Holding Companies and Change in Bank Control.* Governs the bank and nonbank expansion of bank holding companies, the divestiture of impermissible nonbank interests, the acquisition of a bank by individuals, and the establishment and activities of financial holding companies.
Z	*Truth in Lending.* Prescribes uniform methods for computing the cost of credit for disclosing credit terms and for resolving errors on certain types of credit accounts. The amendments in 2001 added provisions to implement the Home Ownership and Equity Protection Act of 1994.
AA	*Unfair or Deceptive Acts or Practices.* Establishes consumer complaint procedures and defines unfair or deceptive practices in extending credit to consumers.
CC	*Availability of Funds and Collection of Checks.* Establishes availability schedules, as provided in the EFAA, under which depository institutions must make funds deposited into transaction accounts available for

EXHIBIT 8.4 CONTINUED

Regulation	Title
	withdrawal. The regulation also provides that depository institutions must disclose their funds availability policies to their customers. In addition, Regulation CC establishes rules designed to speed the collection and return of checks and imposes a responsibility on banks to return unpaid checks expeditiously. The provisions of Regulation CC govern all checks, not just those collected through the Federal Reserve System.
DD	*Truth in Savings.* Requires depository institutions to provide disclosures to enable consumers to make meaningful comparisons on deposit accounts.

Source: The Federal Reserve Board: Regulations, May 15, 2002.

Account Balances

Any idle balances in bank DDAs are assigned an earnings credit allowance or rate (ECR) in lieu of the direct payment of interest (due to Reg Q), based on the three-month U.S. Treasury Bill rate. The ECR calculation that follows in Exhibit 8.5 assumes an ECR of 2.5 percent, which was typical during the late 1990s. Although each bank uses its own account analysis format, the top portion of the account analysis is often organized as described in the following subsections.

Cash Management Service Charges

The cash management portion of the account analysis will vary by bank. Depending on the variety of services used, this section can be several pages long. An illustrative configuration is shown in Exhibit 8.6.

The last line, *net due for services,* is significant because a company must pay the bank this amount as a fee for cash management products

EXHIBIT 8.5

Illustrative Balance Presentation in Bank Account Analysis Statement

Description	Definition	Illustrative Amount
Average *ledger* balance	Average daily balance based on the ledger sum of debits and credits; does not reflect funds that can be used immediately by the account holder.	$230,110
Less: Average *float*	Average funds in the process of collection through assigned availability.	−$208,173
Equals: Average *collected* balance	Average funds that are usable for transactions or investments, the bank having received funds settlement.	$21,937
Less: Reserve requirement (currently 10%)	The amount set by the Federal Reserve to support the banking system's liquidity. This amount cannot be lent to borrowers and does not earn an ECR credit.	−$2,194
Equals: Average earning balance	The amount on which the corporate customer earns an ECR credit.	$19,743
ECR (earnings credit rate)	An interest allowance against positive balances in a corporate DDA, often pegged to the 91-day U.S. Treasury Bill rate.	2.5%
ECR allowance	The calculated dollar earnings credit amount.	* $41

*Using an ECR allowance of 2.5 percent, calculated as ($19,743) × (.025) ÷ (12)

EXHIBIT 8.6

Illustrative Cash Management Service Presentation in Bank Account Analysis Statement

Service	Reference	Quantity	Unit Price	Price Extension
Account maintenance	1	2	$20.00	$40
Deposits—unencoded	2A	140	$0.18	$25
Deposits—encoded	2B	600	$0.12	$72
Returned items	3	50	$3.00	$150
Checks paid	4	400	$0.18	$72
ACH debits/credits	5	100	$0.15	$15
Fedwires	6	4	$12.00	$48
Total charges	7			$422
Net due for services	8			$381

References:

1. *Account maintenance* is the fixed charge assessed to cover the bank's overhead costs associated with a DDA.
2. *Deposits* are checks presented for deposit. *Unencoded* checks do not have the dollar amount encoded in the MICR line; *encoded* checks have been imprinted by the corporate depositor with the dollar amount using an encoding machine. Encoded checks usually have a lower unit price.
3. *Returned items* are checks not honored by the drawee bank, either due to insufficient funds or a stopped payment by the maker.
4. *Checks paid* are disbursements written against the account.
5. *ACH debits/credits* are automated clearing house debits and credits to the account.
6. *Fedwires* are same-day electronic transfers of funds through the Federal Reserve System.
7. *Total charges* are the sum of the price extensions for all cash management services.
8. *Net due for services* is the difference between total charges and the ECR allowance based on the balances in the account.

used. Companies are effectively charged in two forms for bank services: the balances left on deposit and the fee for services. In this example, the company pays by leaving an average of $22,000 in collected balances and a fee of $381.

The Real Cost
of Leaving Balances

The economic cost of banking is far greater than the explicit charge of $422 (reference 7, in Exhibit 8.6), because the balances left on deposit should be valued at the company's cost of capital. Assuming 12 percent as the cost of capital, the balances are valued at $220 (12 percent ÷ 12 months × $22,000). With the fees of $382, the total implicit monthly banking cost is $602, about 30 percent higher! The real cost of leaving balances at the bank is so significant that the cash management function should devote a major effort to reducing them to nearly zero.

Using the Account Analysis to Review Cash Management

The account analysis is more than an invoice and a monitor of balance activity. It is also a report to treasury on banking products used, which should be carefully reviewed to determine if the optimal mix of services have been selected. The following 10 suggestions can help improve usage of cash management services and eliminate unnecessary expenses.

Collections

Here are three collection ideas.

1. *If funds are collected in field offices, review where those funds are deposited.* Using a local bank branch may be convenient, but the deposit may be too late in the day for same-day ledger credit. Most banks have early branch cut-off times, because their courier makes one stop each day at the branch (see the discussion in Chapter 3). One solution to the problem is to deposit where there are later closing times, such as at the main bank or the operations center. Remember, one day missed on an average $15,000

Review of Bank Charges

Unless large balances are left in the account, the typical ECR allowance provides minimal relief for a company using several bank services. Furthermore, each service has a bank-specific definition. Request a glossary of terms used from your bank and ask for assistance in understanding and evaluating each charge.

Banks occasionally make mistakes in constructing the account analysis:

- Charges may be incurred for services that have been discontinued.

- Banks may fail to apply the correct price per transaction.

- Volumes may be in error. Some volumes can be tracked relatively easily:

  - The number of deposits and checks deposits can be traced from deposit tickets.

  - Wire transfer activity can be verified from wire logs.

  - The approximate volume of disbursements can be calculated from the check register, by comparing the first and last check numbers issued in a month. This assumes that the number of outstanding checks will be similar over time.

If uncertain of the appropriateness of any bank charge, ASK!

deposit for each field office account is worth $1,500 a year (at a 10 percent cost of capital).

2. *If bank lockboxes are used, carefully examine how the bank processes mail, the check deposit, and the transmission of daily activity.* Lockbox costs add up quickly, and some of the current unbundled charges may not be required to efficiently manage the work. Here are some examples:

- Review the standard operating instructions to reduce the occurrence of exception processing, which can cause higher fees; for example, allow checks within $5 of the invoice amount to be deposited, and resolve the difference later with the customer; accept any name on the payee ("pay to the order of") line.

- Ask the bank to review the deposit schedule to optimize availability. Don't require multiple deposits if one captures most of the daily activity.

- Decide whether extra check copies are really needed, or the stapling of check copies to remittance documents, or courier delivery of remittance documents, or any other service that may not significantly impact accounting activities.

3. *If collection flows haven't been reengineered recently, consider having the entire lockbox workflow imaged by the bank or a vendor.* This will force a reexamination of how the current process works and will ultimately provide same-day electronic file delivery of lockbox receipts. It may be determined that the invoice design needs to be streamlined, or that the mailing address can be confused with the company address, or that there are too many requests for payment (e.g., invoice, monthly statement, reminder notice), or that there are other collection inefficiencies.

Concentration

Here are three concentration ideas:

1. *If more than 20 bank accounts are maintained, examine why these accounts are open.* Companies often have idle accounts that are infrequently used. Balances may be moved into an account earning a higher return, then the idle accounts can be closed, saving the monthly maintenance charge and other fees. Assuming the balances are $5,000, each idle bank account closed is worth about $1,000 a year ($600 for the value of the earnings + $400 a year for the maintenance and other charges).

2. *If a sweep investment product is used (see Chapter 5), it may be more cost-effective to leave balances to earn the ECR rate, given the historic upward slope of the yield curve.* ECRs are tied to the 91-day Treasury Bill rate, and in mid-2002 were earning about 1.5 percent. A sweep costs about $150 a month but yields only about 3 percent. Assuming a daily balance of $5,000, the incremental 1.5 percent earned is worth only $75 a year ($5,000 × 1.5 percent). The sweep would actually *cost* $1,725 ($150 × 12 months − $75).

3. *If a credit line is constantly being used for working capital, move money back to the lender whenever there is an excess of cash, to minimize interest costs.*

- When the same bank is used for credit and cash management services, excess funds can repay borrowing through an intrabank transfer based on standing instructions. These transfers cost about 50 cents, and can move on a same-day basis.

- When different banks are used for credit and cash management services, develop a cash forecast of inflows and outflows, and keep a reasonable balance in the bank to cover emergencies. Move funds back to lenders through a PC terminal-based ACH transfer for next-day credit.

Disbursement

Here are four disbursement ideas:

1. *If information is known the previous day on the next day's wires, consider terminal-based ACH the previous day.* The company may be using Fedwires for loan repayments, to make deposits into employee savings programs (such as 401ks), for tax payments, or for major vendor disbursements (such as a progress payment on a construction project). These are all suitable applications for ACH payments. Most banks will allow ACHs to be released until late in the afternoon, allowing funds to be transferred for next-day settlement. As ACHs cost about 1 percent of Fedwires, there can be a significant savings.

2. *If the bank's full reconciliation service has not been selected, reexamine this decision, particularly if the positive pay product is used.* A daily-issued file is already being sent to the bank for matching against clearing items, so the bank has the necessary data to provide full recon. The additional charge averages about 4 cents an item, while partial recon (a listing of cleared items that must be manually reconciled), which the company is likely receiving, costs about 2 cents per item. The incremental 2-cent cost is far below likely internal accounting costs.

3. *If purchasing cards are not being used, probably far too much is being spent on each buying decision.* Studies indicate that each buying cycle, including the purchase order, the receiving report, and the payment, costs between $50 and $100. Purchasing cards cost about $1 to $2 per transaction and have various safeguards embedded in the card to prevent misuse or fraud. Your credit card company or your bank can explain how the product works.

4. *If checks and other vendor disbursements are being issued, consider comprehensive payables (discussed in Chapter 4).* A payment cycle averages about $5 per transaction, while banks are bidding the product at about 50 cents (plus postage). A company issuing 2,000

TIPS & TECHNIQUES

Analysis of Current System

A good approach to reviewing cash management fees is to carefully examine every account analysis item. Each charge should be examined to determine whether it is required in the conduct of your business. Have the bank explain the services used, and inquire whether there might not be a better approach. In bidding banking business (as discussed in Chapter 9), carefully explain, itemize, and diagram the current system, and ask the bidders to suggest the optimal system. A fresh look can be worth hundreds of thousands of dollars each year!

nonpayroll disbursements a month would save some $100,000 annually!

The Uniform Commercial Code (UCC)

One of the other formative influences on the U.S. business-banking environment is the Uniform Commercial Code (UCC). The UCC is a set of regulations covering commercial transactions adopted by the individual states, sometimes in a slightly different form. Drafted in 1953, it was originally designed to cover paper-based payments, but in recent years has been expanded to address large-dollar electronic funds transfers as well. The UCC defines the rights and duties of the parties in commercial transactions and provides a statutory definition of commonly used business practices. The articles that are most relevant to the cash manager are:

- *Article 3—Negotiable instruments.* This article was designed to cover paper instruments and checks in particular. The article defines what constitutes payment in full and the liabilities of the parties in the event of unauthorized signatures.

- *Article 4—Bank deposits and collections.* This article defines the roles and responsibilities of the parties involved in the deposit and collection process. It determines the obligations of both the bank and the company in conducting business, including the company's obligation to inform the bank of any unauthorized signatures and to examine bank statements within 30 days of the statement being sent.

- *Article 4A—Funds transfer.* This statute addresses the responsibilities and duties of the parties involved in electronic funds transfers, which includes Fedwire, CHIPS, and ACH. The major provisions concern the security procedures that are made available to customers when making electronic transfers. It specifically deals with the issue of bank and customer liability and protects banks from consequential damages for losses incurred as a result of a bank error.

- *Article 5—Letters of credit.* This section defines the roles, responsibilities, and obligations of parties engaged in commercial letters of credit that require documentary drafts or documentary demands for payment. It does not cover standby letters of credit.

Summary

The history of U.S. banking legislation helps to explain how the banking environment evolved and the priority placed on cash management. The collection and mobilization of funds through multiple layers of banks, the management of idle balances, and reliance on payment by check are legacies of the banking laws and the Glass-Steagall Act. Deregulation of the industry is still too recent to have fundamentally changed the complexity of the collection and disbursement process in the United States.

CASE STUDY

Bill Fold was able to help his colleagues understand the U.S. banking environment. Bill and Ann reviewed the nature of the different types of financial institutions, the structure and the role of the central bank, and the major legislation and regulations that have shaped the banking industry. Bill's associates could now appreciate why the complexity of the multilayered payment system, combined with the geographical expanse covered, required sophisticated tools and vehicles to manage cash flows efficiently.

CHAPTER 9

Bank Relationship Management

After reading this chapter, you will be able to

- Recognize current trends in relationship banking
- Appreciate the purpose and use of the request-for-information (RFI) and request-for-proposal (RFP)
- Understand the evaluation and scoring of bank proposals
- Consider issues relating to the pricing of cash management services
- Review your relationship and transaction bank contacts and activities

CASE STUDY

Treasurer Bill Fold has been pleased with the cooperation of his bankers throughout the review of his treasury management operations. However, he now realizes that various changes have occurred in the financial services environment that will continue to affect his company. He knows that deregulation may make access to credit more difficult and that his cash management business may have to be awarded to his credit banks to retain their goodwill. Bill plans to meet with his cash managers, Ann and Rick, to develop a comprehensive approach to bank relationship management.

Bank relationship management is a comprehensive approach to the bank-corporate partnership, involving all of the credit and non-credit services offered by financial institutions and required by their corporate customers. Noncredit services are all of the for-fee products offered to corporate customers, including cash management, trust, shareholder services, custody, trade finance, foreign exchange, and derivative instruments. Elements of relationship management include:

- Sufficient credit arrangements to meet short- and longer-term financing requirements
- Appropriate cash management services for U.S. and global transactions
- Reasonable pricing
- Acceptable service quality
- Consideration for financial institution risk, due to changes in ownership structure, failure, or other outcomes

The period of restrictions on interstate banking and on financial service expansion ended in the latter part of the 1990s. Prior to that time, companies often had relationships with several banks, to provide various credit and noncredit services. To some extent, it was a "buyer's market," with bankers selling their products through every possible marketing device, including, but not limited to:

- Constant calling to build brand recognition
- Entertainment to build personal contact and a sense of "obligation"
- Aggressive pricing, often at or even below fully loaded costs
- A regular rollout of new product offerings
- The intertwining of the bank's systems with the company's systems, to make separation as difficult as possible

Twenty-First-Century Relationship Management

The traditional bank calling strategy worked as long as the banks could generate adequate revenues from all of their corporate business, particularly as most financial institutions had a poor understanding of profitability by customer or product line. Furthermore, commercial banks were restricted in the use of capital, and could not pursue more lucrative business, such as investment banking or insurance.

The changing regulatory environment (discussed in Chapter 8) allows banks and other financial service companies to consider a much broader range of business opportunities, reducing their reliance on credit products and marginally profitable cash management services. Like all for-profit shareholder-owned companies, banks require a reasonable return on equity from each customer, and may terminate a relationship if there is little prospect of acceptable returns in the long run. A proactive relationship management plan is necessary for companies to satisfy their bankers, and for bankers to justify the business "partnership" to their management.

Transaction Banking

Until there is true interstate banking in the United States, a need will continue to exist for transactional bank accounts for local needs. Branch offices may require nearby depositories for various reasons:

- The depositing of checks received in payment of invoices, for the convenience of local customers
- Assistance with local banking requirements such as coin and currency
- "Accommodation" loans to staff, such as for mortgages or automobile purchases
- Payments on local checks to area vendors or for emergencies
- The cashing of payroll checks

Banking for Branch Employees

While transaction banking is an accommodation for branch employees, the controls developed for these accounts tend to be significantly weaker than for home office accounts. As a result, the fraudulent use of funds in these accounts is a significant concern, particularly as auditors infrequently review procedures, signatories and sources, and uses of funds. It is strongly suggested that branches have access to no more than one local bank, that only two or three senior managers have signing authority; and, whenever possible, that multipurpose account structures be avoided. (A multipurpose account can receive deposits and interbank transfers and can issue disbursements for local purchases.)

These situations require transaction accounts near the field office and are not intended as substitutes for relationship banking. There are also regulations in certain states that force the use of local accounts; for example, California requires that employees be paid with checks drawn on a bank located within the state.

Considerations in Bank Selection

Bank contact has traditionally been through the treasurer, whose responsibilities include the safeguarding of the cash and near-cash assets of the company. In recent years, access has been extended through other business functions, as banks have broadened their product offerings. Too often, treasury staff remains unaware of the resulting dilution of its responsibility.

- Purchasing and accounts payable is often the entry for EDI, e-commerce, purchasing cards, and disbursement outsourcing (comprehensive payables).

- The payroll or human resources department may invite discussions concerning the direct deposit of payroll and payroll ATM cards.

- The investment or real estate department may be interested in such specialized services as stock loan, custody, and escrow or tax services.

- Systems or information technology (IT) often initiates discussions about any of the more technology-oriented bank services.

Given the current credit environment, it is essential that treasury be the gatekeeper for all financial institution contact. This will assure that an attractive package of profitable business is assembled for the relationship banks and to prevent unauthorized negotiations or contracting between the company and other banks.

The RFI

In establishing a comprehensive bank relationship strategy, an initial step used by many companies is to issue a request-for-information (RFI) letter to candidate financial institutions. The RFI is used to determine which banks are qualified and interested in providing banking services. A list of potential bank bidders can be developed from previous calling efforts; contacts at conferences and meetings; and referrals from accountants, attorneys, and business colleagues. (Note: The procedures described throughout this chapter may be applied to the selection of nonbank vendors; see, for example, the discussion of treasury information systems in Chapter 6).

The RFI letter should explain the purpose and intention of the company in establishing a long-term banking relationship(s) for credit and cash management services. Basic descriptive and financial data is provided, including contact names, business locations, credit requirements, volumes of current services, technology used in financial transactions, and other relevant information. The letter should then solicit indications of interest in bidding on the services required by the company.

Questions might be phrased as follows:

- Is your institution interested in being considered as the relationship bank for the company?

- Do you provide the various credit and cash management services we require?

- What is the history of your bank in providing these services? At which locations are the services offered?

- What is your bank's expectation in terms of being awarded business for the relationship to be sufficiently attractive and profitable?

Be certain to specify a response date, and provide contact names and telephone numbers for follow-up questions and contacts.

The responses to the RFI are used to select the banks to be included in the request-for-proposal process. This determination is usually based on demonstrated competence in cash management services, a commitment to providing credit, and a clear desire for a long-term relationship.

The RFP

The request-for-proposal (RFP) process has been federal government practice for decades. Companies began using RFPs in the early 1990s to formalize a purchasing decision that had become too casual. Existing bank and vendor relationships tended to be given extensions of old business and any new opportunities under consideration without a formal bidding process. The Association for Financial Professionals (AFP) (*www.afponline.org*) supported the RFP process by publishing three volumes of *Standardized RFPs* beginning in 1996. Volume 1 services are available through the Web site for a standard fee for each RFP. Volumes 2 and 3 can be purchased in a printed book, which includes an electronic version (on 3.5-inch disk in Microsoft Word).

Services for which RFP templates are available include the following:

Volume 1: "Domestic Services"	Controlled Disbursement
	Depository Services
	Wholesale Lockbox
	Wire Transfer
	ACH
	EDI
	Information Reporting
Volume 2: "Domestic Services"	Disbursement Outsourcing
	Treasury Workstations
	Purchasing Cards
	Merchant Card Services
	Retail Lockbox
	Custody
Volume 3: "Global Services"	Account Structure
	Depository and Collections Services
	Liquidity Management
	Global Funds Transfer
	Electronic Banking and Information Reporting
	Foreign Exchange

The original desire to extend bidding opportunities to banks and vendors outside of the relationship group has changed significantly in the past few years. The lifting of interstate banking restrictions (discussed in Chapter 8) and disappearing credit (see Chapter 10) has forced treasurers to concentrate their banking, with fewer financial institutions, ending the process of bank selection based on price or technology. The current emphasis is on meeting the bank's need for adequate profitability, outsourcing noncore activities, and finding relationships that can provide most or all of the necessary functions at a fair price for services received.

Issues Covered in Bank RFPs

The request-for-proposal (RFP) is usually organized as lists of questions pertaining to general banking concerns and to specific attributes relating to each service. Specific conditions for contracting for services are included in the RFP; examples are given in Exhibit 9.1.

EXHIBIT 9.1

Conditions for Contracting for Services

Logistics of Proposal	1. Provide your best and final bid. 2. Submit the bid no later than a specified date and time. 3. Provide X copies of the bid in print and/or electronic format.
Bidder Authorization	1. An authorized bank officer must sign proposals. 2. The signed bid constitutes a binding commitment should the bank be awarded the business.
Date of Award	1. The company expects to award the business by September 1, 200X. 2. The company retains the right to reject all bids.
Nondiscrimination Clause	1. The bank agrees not to discriminate against any employee or applicant for employment with respect to race, sex, religion, ancestry, age, physical appearance, or handicap. 2. Any violation of this covenant may be regarded as a material breach of the contract.
Confidentiality	1. The bank agrees to hold in confidence any data provided by the company in this RFP or in relation to this RFP that are not otherwise publicly available. 2. The bank will not use any confidential material for any purpose unrelated to this RFP without written approval of the company.
Other Possible Conditions	1. Contract duration and cancellation. 2. Modification of the bid during final negotiations. 3. Standard company contracts and purchasing authorization(s). 4. Costs incurred by banks in preparing bids. 5. Use of subcontractors by the bank. 6. Bidder questions about the RFP.

General Issues

General issues pertain to any cash management service being considered and apply to the bank's financial stability and creditworthiness, approach to management of the organization for and delivery of services, and similar issues. Typical questions and data required are provided in Exhibit 9.2.

Specific Cash Management Issues

The issues pertaining to each cash management service will of course vary by product. Some examples are provided in Exhibit 9.3.

Review of Pricing

Although pricing has long been *the* consideration in selecting a domestic cash management bank, recent experience has seen a decline in its importance.

- *Maturity of the product cycle.* Because many cash management products are in the mature phase of the product cycle, there is minimal variation in the price charged by most banks. Furthermore, information on pricing is published in the *Phoenix-Hecht Blue Book of Pricing* (*www.phoenixhecht.com/*), making pricing data fairly widely available to all interested parties.

- *Unbundling.* Banks have unbundled pricing for cash management, making line-by-line comparisons meaningless. Some banks charge for each specific service, while others include the service in the fee for the underlying product. For example, controlled disbursing may include positive pay or may be priced separately.

- *Quality.* It is generally recognized that any quality or service problems relating to a specific cash management product can cost many times the price per unit of the service. As a result, the savings of a few cents per item is not important when compared to the cost to resolve an error, a communication or transmission problem, or other bank failures.

EXHIBIT 9.2

Bank RFP Questions: General Issues

Financial Stability and Creditworthiness	1. Identify key measures of the bank's financial strength, (e.g., capital ratios, market capitalization, total assets).
	2. Provide ratings for the bank and/or bank holding company from two of the major credit rating agencies.
	3. Provide audited financial statements.
Organization	1. List names, titles, phone and fax numbers, e-mail address, and brief biographies of bank contact personnel.
	2. Will one primary contact be assigned to the account? If so, from which area of the organization? How many employees does the bank have in key areas providing the service?
Commitment to the Product	1. What differentiates your service from other providers?
	2. How do you plan to keep this product current and competitive? What approach is the bank taking in the development of new services?
Disaster Recovery	1. Describe your disaster recovery facilities and plans. If these facilities are maintained by a third party, explain how you expect to recover processing capability in the event of a disaster.
	2. Has your bank experienced a disaster? How was the situation handled?
Quality Assurance	1. Do you maintain quality standards, including minimal and target performance goals?
	2. Do you periodically publish a quality chartbook and/or allow customer access to quality review meetings?
References	1. Provide three references in our industry or with similar processing requirements.
	2. Provide the names of two companies that have ceased doing cash management business with your bank in the last year.

Specific Terms
Offered by Lenders

Credit facilities are normally not bid through an RFP, but are simply requested of the financial institution based on past and projected financial statements, a business plan, booked and anticipated sales, and other relevant data. Specific terms offered by lenders include the following:

- Amount of the loan

- Maturity or duration of the loan

- Interest rate, usually the prime rate or LIBOR plus or minus one or more percent

- Payment schedule, usually monthly

- Collateral pledged to secure the loan, usually involving a perfected first security interest in:

  - Leasehold improvements

  - Accounts receivable

  - Inventory

  - Equipment, furniture, and fixtures

- Periodic financial statements (usually quarterly) that present the company's financial position and support the loan

- Financial covenants that the company must meet, usually specified as the attainment of minimum balance sheet account and ratio results; for example:

  - A typical balance sheet account minimum is net worth above $500,000 or some other amount

  - A typical ratio minimum is net worth-to-total liabilities greater than 2:1

- Material adverse change clause, which terminates the loan should the company's financial condition significantly change

---

EXHIBIT 9.3

Bank RFP Questions: Cash Management Services

Wholesale Lockbox

1. List the bank's schedule for post office pickups of wholesale lockbox mail for weekdays, weekends, and holidays.
2. Does the bank have a unique five-digit zip code assigned exclusively for receipt of wholesale lockbox items?
3. Who performs the fine sort per box number, the bank or the post office? If the bank sorts the lockbox mail, describe the mail-sorting operation. Include manual and automated handling, ability to read barcodes, and peak volume capabilities.

Controlled Disbursement

1. Cite the published time at which customers are notified of their daily controlled disbursement clearings.
2. What was the average daily notification time during the previous quarter?
3. How many notifications are made each day?
4. If more than one notification is made, what percent of the dollars and items was included in each notification during the previous quarter?

ACH

1. Describe the procedures used to verify accurate and secure receipt of transmissions.
2. Can the bank automatically redeposit items returned for insufficient or uncollected funds? When items are redeposited, are any entries posted to the customer's account?
3. What are the hardware/software requirements for PC-based services? Does the application support use of a LAN? Will assistance with software installation be provided?

Drafting Company-specific RFPs

Access to electronic versions of RFPs has greatly eased the process of drafting questions and assuring that important matters are covered. However, many users simply copy and paste from the files in the AFP books, rather than thoughtfully edit to exclude irrelevant material or write new, company-specific questions. Furthermore, it is important to include information germane to the company, such as volumes, peak processing days, technology constraints, design of remittance documents, interest in outsourcing, and similar issues. Remember: A full set of RFP responses with accompanying technical specifications and promotional material can print out to 1,000 pages!

Review of Pro Forma Account Analyses

The account analysis is the monthly invoice treasury receives for banking services (see Chapter 8). There are three purposes in conducting a pro forma (or projected) account analysis.

1. *Product pricing.* It is useful to calculate the complete cost of each cash management product and to determine if any unusual fees are being charged. Exhibit 9.4 illustrates one bank's bid for wholesale lockbox services as an element of a comprehensive relationship plan. The account analysis pricing shows a per-item charge of 43 cents, but the total cost per item is $1.48 (calculated as $7,709 total monthly charges ÷ 5,200 items)! The compilation of such data permits the determination of all ancillary costs for each cash management service.

2. *Format.* Another consideration in developing a pro forma account analysis is that the format and peculiarities of each bank's pricing can be identified. Remember: If the account analysis cannot be easily understood, you will either fail to determine that all

EXHIBIT 9.4

Lockbox Account Analysis Detail

Component Cost	Quantity	Per-Item Charge	Total Charge
Wholesale maintenance	5	$100.00	$500.00
Lockbox deposit preparation	100	$1.25	$125.00
Deposit ticket	100	$0.80	$80.00
Wholesale item, photo	5,200	$0.43	$2,236.00
Nondepositable item	1,000	$0.25	$250.00
Data transmission—box 1	1	$100.00	$100.00
Data transmission—boxes 2–5	4	$40.00	$160.00
Keystrokes	23,000	$0.01	$230.00
Per-image scanned	12,000	$0.03	$360.00
Image output per CD-ROM	8	$15.00	$120.00
Image services per item	12,000	$0.27	$3,240.00
Deposited items—on-us	400	$0.01	$4.00
Deposited items—in district cities	1,600	$0.05	$80.00
Deposited items—other in-district	1,600	$0.06	$96.00
Deposited items—out of district	1,600	$0.08	$128.00
Total monthly charge			$7,709.00

charges are valid or will spend considerable time in trying to analyze the fees charged each month.

3. *Balance information.* The account analysis presents all relevant balance information, including ledger (book) balances, collected and available balances, and earnings credit rate (ECR) allowances (see Chapter 8). Despite the trend toward standardization, there may be variations in these calculations due to bank-specific practices.

Evaluation of the RFPs

Because of the sheer number of potential questions and answers in a set of proposals, it is very difficult to simply read through and make any sense of the material. For this reason, one technique has proven helpful:

TIPS & TECHNIQUES

Helpful Hint for Organizing RFP Data

A comprehensive proposal can be more than 1,000 pages long, including accompanying exhibits and explanations of services offered. If RFPs are sent to just three banks, that's 3,000 pages of reading! Consider having the banks send one printed copy of their proposal for reference and another in an electronic file so that relevant data can be copied into a table, compared, and analyzed.

to organize each set of responses into a table, listing the bank names in the columns and the important answers in the rows.

Exhibit 9.5 presents an excerpt from such a table, created for lock-box proposals from four banks. A complete table involving many of the responses could be several pages long. Note the variation in the responses to the RFP questions.

Measures of Performance

It is next necessary to array the responses for each question, with the intention of assigning points based on a template of average answers. For example, a question may be asked concerning the typical time for the implementation of a lockbox. The bank responses can range from 4 weeks to 12 weeks. The point assignment could be as follows:

2 points:	4–6 weeks
1 point:	7–10 weeks
0 points:	11 or more weeks

Despite the maturity of cash management products, there are often significant differences in the responses. The application of points to these RFP answers allows for the objective ranking of each bank.

EXHIBIT 9.5

Selected Responses to Lockbox RFP Questions

	Bank A	Bank B	Bank C	Bank D
Unique zip code	Wholesale and retail share unique	No unique zip codes	Unique for wholesale	Wholesale and retail share unique; retail sorted by barcode
Number of mail pickups at post office	10 daily; 5 weekend	3 daily; 1 weekend	19 daily; 7 weekend	7 daily; 4 weekend
Quality assurance program	Monthly customer tracking for 30 types of errors	Monthly consolidated tracking for 12 types of errors	Tracking only for holdover, investigations, productivity	Full program: customer tracking, chartbooks, open customer meetings
Customer service	Primary representative and pool support	Specialist and pool support	Team (specialist for each service)	Pool; no specific assignments
Error rate per 10,000 transactions	1.2	1.8	<10 (vague answer)	0.6
Availability assignment	By item	Float factor used for retail lockbox	By item with fractional availability	Option of float factor or by item
Volume for price discount	At 20,000/ month	At 50,000/ month	No stated discounts	At 25,000/ month
Period of price guarantee	1 year standard; second year available	1 year with inflation increases for second year	2 years	1 year; no guarantees thereafter

Weighted Scoring of Proposals

The final step in evaluating the banks' proposals is to assign weights to each response based on the perceived importance of the question. The total weight should add to 100 percent, but any individual question could have a weighting ranging from a value of 0 percent to as much as 15 or 20 percent. The weights are based on the company's perception of the importance of each question.

An illustrative weighted scoring for lockbox is provided in Exhibit 9.6 for the four banks from Exhibit 9.5. The responses are displayed as unweighted—that is, the raw point assignments—and weighted, with the value specified for each response applied to the point assignment. The final results show that Bank A, with 247 points, and Bank D, with 242 points, are significantly better than Banks B and C.

These scores allow the company to consider whether the expected results are consistent with the analysis or if some adjustment in the weightings is necessary. Should the results stand, the company can visit the two finalists to ask difficult questions, meet the client team assigned by each bank, and develop a sense that the bank wants to be a long-term "partner." Contact all references, and probe to see if the bank has met its service obligations with its other clients.

Guidelines for Managing the RFP Process

There are various lessons to be learned in managing the RFP process, for both companies and banks, displayed in Exhibit 9.7.

Managing Your Banking Relationships

Once the decision has been made, the next activity is to review the contracts your bank(s) will require as an essential part of the relationship. Each service is governed by agreements that address the various obligations and requirements of each party, to protect both the bank and the

EXHIBIT 9.6

Evaluation Score Sheet for Lockbox

		Unweighted Scores				Weighted Scores			
	Weight (%)	Bank A	Bank B	Bank C	Bank D	Bank A	Bank B	Bank C	Bank D
Unique zip code	12	2	0	2	3	24	0	24	36
Number of mail pickups at post office	12	2	1	3	2.5	24	12	36	30
Quality assurance program	22	2.5	2	1	3	55	44	22	66
Customer service	16	3	2	2	1	48	32	32	16
Error rate per 10,000 transactions	14	2	1.5	0	3	28	21	0	42
Availability assignment	8	3	2	2.5	3	24	16	20	24
Volume for price discount	8	3	1	0	2.5	24	8	0	20
Period of price guarantee	8	2.5	2	3	1	20	16	24	8
Total Weighted Points	100					247	149	158	242

company in the event of a dispute. The contracts have been drafted by the bank's attorneys, and are based on long-standing precedent as established in the federal banking statutes and the Uniform Commercial Code adopted by all states.

Service-Level Agreements (SLAs)

Service-level agreements cover terms of service for each cash management product, and will vary depending on specific operating issues.

EXHIBIT 9.7

Lessons for Managing the RFP Process

Companies	Banks
1. Make sure that all affected business units are involved in the RFP process.	1. Reply to *all* questions by writing responsive answers.
2. Quality, experience, and concern for the relationship should be as important as price.	2. Proofread the bid for format, font, grammar, and the name of the company, including the footnote.
3. Send the RFPs to banks that have clearly demonstrated they can provide the required services.	3. Make sure that junior bid-writers have all critical data. Ideally, they should participate in the calling effort.
4. Edit the RFP questions so that only the important questions are included. Be certain to include appropriate company data on volumes, processing requirements, and other concerns.	4. Meet the stated requirement for the time of submission, and provide contacts in the event that the company has follow-up questions.
5. Reexamine your weightings once the first set of scores are calculated, to determine if you have assigned the appropriate value to each question.	5. Try to determine if the company has a political agenda, such as the intention to reward a credit line bank with cash management business.

Banks specify standard processing arrangements for the price that is quoted; any variation is considered as an exception, resulting in additional charges. Typical concerns include acceptable and unacceptable payee names on checks for lockbox, names of initiators and approvers

TIPS & TECHNIQUES

Keeping Banking Agreements Updated

Assign the task of updating banking agreements to a specific manager. Treasury staff is often lax in performing this duty. For example, many companies fail to delete approved signatures from their bank's records, even though an employee may have long departed the company. Or lockbox requirements may change, such as new company names or the preferred processing of nonstandard items (such as non-U.S. dollar checks), but no one informs the bank. It is important to keep this information up to date, to protect the company *and* the bank.

for wire transfers, approved account signatories, and approved users and access restrictions for treasury information systems.

The bank requires these documents to instruct it on how to handle any transactions that are initiated and to protect itself in the event of a dispute or attempted fraud. Furthermore, the bank will require its customers to indemnify and hold it harmless from and against any liability, loss, or costs arising from each service provided.

Relationship Reviews

Given the partnership orientation of banks and companies, there has been a growing trend toward periodic relationship reviews. The objectives of the review are to:

- Assure that the relationship is profitable to the bank while providing added value to the company
- Develop a consultative attitude between the bank and the company to improve current processes and increase efficiencies

- Deliver quality customer service and the timely implementation of new products and services
- Understand the future requirements of the company

The review is typically supported by a document discussing the expectations of each party during the coming period, usually one year, and supported by specific calendar targets. For example, it may be agreed that a new cash management service (such as lockbox) will be implemented by October 1. A typical annual review cycle might consist of the following:

- *First quarter.* Formal meeting of company management and bank officers to
    - Discuss the strategic and financial results for the previous year
    - Outline the next year's goals and objectives
    - Schedule the implementation of new initiatives
- *Second quarter.* Calling by the bank's relationship manager to
    - Update the company on service and technology initiatives
    - Introduce product specialists
- *Third quarter.* Informal meeting of company management and bank officers to
    - Review the status of the year's goals
    - Determine which initiatives to emphasize to meet critical objectives
- *Fourth quarter.* Senior-level social event to
    - Discuss current year
    - Plan for the next year and beyond

At each stage in the cycle, adjustments can be made by either party to meet the requirements of the "partnership."

Some companies provide "report cards" to their banks during these meetings, citing statistics on errors, operational quality, customer service assistance, and other factors. However, there has been less use of this approach in recent years due to more pressing obligations of treasury staff. Another factor in the declining popularity of report cards is the reluctance of companies to appear to negatively judge their credit banks. That said, maintaining some sort of records on the bank's performance can be informative during quarterly meetings.

Summary

Relationship banking is no longer a situation where several credit and cash management providers compete for corporate business based on price and service quality. Today, one or two comprehensive bank relationships are becoming the standard, involving all of the financial products and services used by the corporation. This decision often involves using a formal RFP approach to select banks, establish operating procedures, and review current and future activities. Banks seek corporate clients that can provide a stable, long-term, and profitable relationship; companies want a reliable source of credit and quality noncredit services.

CASE STUDY

Bill Fold met with Ann and Rick to consider a comprehensive approach to bank relationship management. Their concern for continuing access to credit and quality cash management services convinced the group to meet with their financial institutions to construct a plan for a future "partnership," rather than acquiring services on an as-needed basis. Each of the banks expressed a desire to participate in such a strategy. However, the Bank of Yesterday demanded all of the company's credit, investment, and noncredit business, while the Bank of Never decided that there simply wasn't enough profit potential to continue the relationship. Bill, Ann, and Rick had several excellent meetings with the Bank of Tomorrow, which showed a genuine interest in a long-term partnership with GETDOE and a concern for a mutually beneficial relationship. After consultation with the CEO and CFO, it was agreed to establish the company's primary banking relationship with that institution.

CHAPTER 10

Future Trends

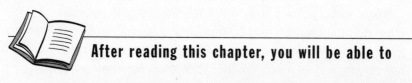

After reading this chapter, you will be able to

- Review the changes occurring in collections and disbursements

- Appreciate concerns relating to banking relationships and credit rationing

- Understand disaster recovery and contingency planning issues

- Evaluate the trends in treasury organization

CASE STUDY

Treasurer Bill Fold has been asked to make a presentation to the board of directors about the changes he anticipates in the treasury organization. E-commerce and the transition to electronic payments are transforming the fundamental business cycle, and the board is concerned about treasury's response to this development and to the credit rationing faced by other companies.

Bill wants to focus on core competencies and minimize the operating costs of finance, especially systems investment in areas that are noncore. The board is anxious to be assured that treasury has anticipated and is prepared to undertake the necessary changes to support these new strategies.

225

Bill was not caught unawares by the board's request, particularly in light of the problems of Enron and Arthur Andersen. For a number of months he has been talking to his industry peers and his banks to assess recent trends and their impact. Significant progress has been made at GETDOE in bringing cash management and banking practices to a reasonable level of efficiency.

Nevertheless, there is concern that the financial services environment is changing so rapidly that current initiatives may be obsolete within a few years. In considering the key developments affecting treasury, Bill, Ann I. Shade, the cash manager and Rick Shaw, the international cash manager, have agreed to systematically compile and disseminate information obtained at conferences, in journals, and through banking contacts, and to develop a proposed plan of action.

A s the Greek philosopher Heraclitus noted nearly 2,000 years ago, "Nothing endures but change." In this chapter, we review the likely trend of changes in cash management and banking, and comment on the actions a prudent treasurer might take.

Cash management is evolving as rapidly as any other area of business. Some of the major influencing factors are:

- E-commerce continues to change the business cycle paradigm.

- Consolidation in corporate banking, a trend for over two decades, shows little sign of abating.

- The quest for efficiencies of scale and cost reductions pushes treasury into greater centralization of functions and increased use of electronic methods for collections and disbursements.

- The prevention of fraud and control and risk management issues override all other treasury concerns.

Trends in Collections

A major cash management trend has been the movement toward use of electronic payment methods. For the first time in almost a decade, the Federal Reserve reported *declines* in the number of checks processed in 2000 and 2001. As often happens, consumers adopt new trends faster than the commercial world. While the United States is still a long way from being a nation that collects and disburses electronically, consumer acceptance of some of the new Internet-based services, and digitization of paper formats, are helping to accelerate the trend.

Electronic Bill Presentment and Payment (EBPP)

According to the Harris Poll of April 17, 2002, mobile and Internet technology is used by over 66 percent of the adult population in the United States. Although buying products on the Internet and using a credit card to pay is a generally accepted practice, the process of viewing and settling the bill electronically, known as electronic bill presentment and payment (EBPP), is not. Nevertheless, the service has applications for many industries, from financial service providers to telecommunications companies and utilities.

With the emergence of secure e-mail and wireless delivery, it is expected that EBPP use will rise dramatically. The Tower Group estimates that by 2005 more than 2.4 billion consumer and B2B payments will be presented electronically.

Electronic Check Presentment (ECP)

ECP is revolutionizing the collection process by capturing data from a check and converting it into an electronic transmission that is cleared through the banking system. This not only accelerates the presentment of clearing items, but also speeds the notification of any checks being returned due to stop payments or insufficient funds in the account of

Electronic Bill Payment

It should not be assumed that because a payment has been initiated through the Internet that the settlement will also be made electronically, logical though that may seem. Some banks debit accounts promptly upon receipt of the payment order and then issue payment by check several days later. This allows a bank to use the float for the intervening time. Anyone using an electronic bill payment service should check with their bank to determine how and when the actual payment will be made, to avoid late payment and penalties.

the payor. In the case of check truncation in the collection process, the paper item often follows the electronic transmission. In point-of-sale situations, the transaction is converted into an ACH item and the check is often returned to the maker for storage or destruction.

Direct Debits

There has been limited, albeit increasing, acceptance of direct debits in the United States. (A direct debit is where the payor has preauthorized the payee to initiate a debit to the payor's account.) Used most notably by federal and state governments since the mid-1980s to collect corporate taxes, direct debits have more recently been promoted by industries where low-value, regular, and frequent payments are due, such as mortgages and insurance premiums. Variable payments, such as phone and utility bills, require that 10 days notice be given to consumers before debiting their accounts. Again, consumers have been faster to adopt this technology than the corporate world.

Direct Debiting for International Collections

An emerging opportunity is in using direct debiting for international collections. With much wider acceptance levels in other parts of the world, especially in Europe, some of the larger global banks now offer collection services using local low-value payment systems for direct debits. This avoids the significantly higher cost of wire transfers or availability delays and foreign exchange exposure created by checks.

Trends in Disbursements

While electronic payments account for only 18 percent of all payments (refer back to Exhibit 2.1), the advantages of disbursement by paper are diminishing.

- ECP has made the clearing process more efficient, eroding some of the clearing float benefits of paper disbursements.

- The willingness of trading partners to negotiate "float-neutral" terms (where the value date of the electronic payment is the same as when a check would have been debited to the payor's account) is reducing resistance through compensation for foregone mail and clearing float.

- The current interest rate environment reduces the value of disbursement float.

- The cost of fraud and of measures to prevent fraud erases many of the pricing advantages of checks.

- B2B e-commerce requires the completion of the transaction by electronic payment.

- Terminal-based ACH is increasingly used for large value, nonurgent payments.

- Payment security over the Internet through such providers as Identrus (*www.identrus.com*) permits identity and credit verification, and provides performance and payment guarantees.

- Electronic cross-border, low-value, batch payment options are being developed to expedite global transactions. Some proprietary products are currently offered by global banks to link these payment systems in several countries. Other initiatives such as STEP2, developed by the Euro Banking Association (EBA), is based on open architecture access.

- The letter-of-credit process has traditionally been paper-intensive and time-consuming. The latest developments by companies such as Bolero.net and Trade Card have automated the process and facilitated electronic initiation and completion of the trade. The entire process can now be achieved in days rather than weeks.

Obviously, checks are not about to disappear tomorrow. Their value continues as a mechanism to "pay anyone, anywhere." Their future will focus on fraud prevention at all four stages of check disbursement—preissuance, issuance, reconciliation, and retention. Imaging technology has assisted in improving the quality of data capture, the timeliness of transmissions, and access to lists of authorized company signers and quick identification of suspected fraudulent activity. Just-in-time printing has resolved many of the issues associated with the safekeeping and issuance of checks.

Banking Relationship Concerns

For 50 years, commercial lending in America was a buyer's market, with many sellers—the U.S. banks—chasing available buyers—their corporate clients. This happens when an industry is experiencing economic competition and there is too much supply of product for the market to absorb. Sellers often cannot make an adequate return on their investment. Corporations were in charge, and banks wined and dined them to sell their wares. Every time a piece of business was put out to bid, a dozen or more banks scrambled to write proposals, cut prices, and promise implementation support, superior customer service, and visits by senior management.

The New Seller's Market in Banking

The ending of interstate banking restrictions and the passage of the Gramm-Leach-Bliley Act (1999) gives banks, securities firms, insurers, and finance companies the freedom to assign capital to any financial service. And as rational managers, they will seek the greatest returns for their shareholders. In fact, past strategies were often suboptimal, in that they were made in the context of severe restrictions on their freedom in assigning capital. Banks had to lend money to corporate customers on terms that were not always attractive, because they were restricted to the banking business.

Commercial banks today are in a seller's market for the financial needs of large corporations. They have the capital to lend or invest, and treasurers must go to them, hat in hand, and ask for consideration. Some banks are turning away borrowers, or are being extremely selective as to the businesses that they will support, while others are demanding higher prices, more revenue, and greater returns. (See, for example, "Who's Getting Hurt by the Loan Drought," *BusinessWeek,* May 20, 2002, pp. 122–123.) Exhibit 10.1 shows returns to the bank when a credit line is used or unused.

The short-term credit in this situation backs the issuance of commercial paper that is accepted practice in that market, because commercial paper is an unsecured instrument. It is obvious that returns are unattractive if credit is the sole piece of business awarded to the bank.

EXHIBIT 10.1

Recent Returns on Credit

	Return on $75-Million Committed Facility		
Credit Facility	**Before Underwriting Expenses**	**After Underwriting Expenses**	**With Noncredit Fee Income**
Is not used	6.75%	3.75%	13.75%
Is used	9.00%	8.20%	10.80%

Assumptions:
1. The borrower is an A-rated credit.
2. The credit facility is a three-year $75-million commitment, $25 million for less than one year and $50 million for three years.
3. Risk-adjusted capital ratios (based on the 1993 Basel Agreement on international lending practices) are used in calculating the capital assigned to each portion of the facility.
4. The bank's cost to underwrite the credit is $30,000.
5. The profit from noncredit fee income is $50,000.
6. Simple interest returns are calculated, rather than internal rate of return (IRR).

Source: Recent data in the *Gold Sheets* (*www.loanpricing.com*), a credit reporting and pricing service. Contact the authors for calculation details.

Three criteria must be met for the bank to earn its cost of capital: if the credit is not used, if the underwriting costs are carefully managed, and, most important, if there is a substantial profit opportunity from fee income.

Capital Rationing

Banks cannot make an adequate return from credit and must support lending with profits from noncredit activities. This was not recognized in the past due to mediocre bank profitability systems and the high returns from cash management and other noncredit products. These factors have changed in recent years: banks now understand their costs, by product, customer, and line of business, and they are seeing dwindling profitability from fee-based business.

Several factors compound the problem for companies, including reduced operating cash flow from the global recession and aftermath of the events of September 11, 2001. Lenders have responded to these developments by supplementing standard contracts with covenants that allow release from funding committed credit lines. Such amendments include "material adverse change" clauses permitting escape if there has been a substantial injurious development in the financial position of the borrower.

Treasurers are facing capital rationing for the first time since the Great Depression. For example, a *Fortune* 500 company with an AA credit rating was recently forced to accept half of its desired credit line needs at more than double the cost of previous facilities. Furthermore, the participating banks demanded, and received, all noncredit fee business at substantially increased pricing; and banks refusing to provide credit lost all of the other business previously enjoyed.

Where Will Banks Use Their Capital?

Alternative uses of bank capital include changing the portfolio of products or investing in U.S. government securities.

- *The product portfolio.* The emphasis on changes in bank product lines will occur as banks focus on more profitable activities, including selected middle-market and small-business lending and noncredit services, credit cards, trust services, and trade finance. There will be an emphasis on developing less capital-intensive electronic delivery methods, such as Web-based applications. Bank capital will also pursue opportunities to diversify, emulating the Citigroup (Citicorp/Travelers) merger (1998) that now includes such companies as Salomon Smith Barney and Associates First Capital.

- *U.S. government securities.* The assets of commercial banks are typically invested as follows: 60 percent in loans and leases, with another 20 percent in investment-grade securities, 5 percent in miscellaneous short-term investments, and 15 percent in non-earning assets. During the decade of the 1990s, the amounts invested in U.S. government securities varied from nearly 18 percent in 1993 to 11.5 percent in early 2002 (according to statistics in monthly issues of the *Federal Reserve Bulletin*, Table 1.26). Banks could decide to invest some of their capital in U.S. government instruments, allowing their balance sheets to return to the safety profile last seen in the early 1990s. (If banks did this, some $375 billion would be removed from lending activity!)

Assume for a moment that a "manageable" amount, say $100 billion, was diverted from normal lending. What is the potential return? Banks lend funds overnight to each other at the federal funds ("Fed funds") rate, which was about 1.80 percent (in mid-2002). At the same time, 10-year U.S. Treasury bonds were yielding about 5.05 percent. A completely safe investment would be the purchase of long bonds funded by Fed funds borrowing, supported by the capital freed from support for corporate lending, as previously discussed. This strategy would result in an annual 3.25 percent gain (that's $3.25 billion for the banks!) without incurring any underwriting or other expense!

Will the Future Bring Systemic Changes?

Throughout the industrial and information ages, our financial system has depended on access to credit, and the free market has generally done an adequate job in assigning funds to creditworthy users. When subsidies have been needed, the government has created various loan guarantee agencies for specific sectors that need support—for example, farming, housing, education, and small business. These situations involve activities deemed essential to our long-term economic security that are unable to compete on a "level playing field" with more robust borrowers.

Now that the capital rationing problem has reached the doors of large corporations, it is unlikely that political support will develop for

Banks' Defensive Strategy

The days of cheap credit are over. Banks have to make enough return on the entire business "partnership" or they will not be interested in the business. A defensive strategy is to:

- Enumerate *all* of the potential business the company has to offer its bankers, and make sure that it's all under the control of the treasury department. In recent years, treasurers more often have been side-stepped; see the discussion in Chapter 9, under "Considerations in Bank Selection" (first few paragraphs). Other financial products that could be included are foreign exchange, derivatives, securities trading, custody, trust and agency services, and the issuance of debt and equity.

- Consider which lenders have the capabilities to provide all or most of the services. Begin discussions with these bankers as to their noncredit revenue requirements for credit business. Consider the relationship history, the competence and interest of the bankers, the breadth of industry experience, and the likelihood that the bank will continue to be interested in providing these services should a merger occur.

- Bid the business in the expectation that the business will be concentrated with no more than one or possibly two banks, effectively excluding all of the others.

governmental solutions. In the absence of *severe* dislocations, treasurers should not realistically expect a resumption of legislated restrictions on banking.

Risk Management

The globalization of economic activity requires treasury to actively participate in the management of business risk. Traditional approaches focus on specific risks: insurance for human or property losses; bank credit lines for short-term liquidity problems; compliance officers and lawyers for regulatory concerns; and security specialists, occupational safety and health advisors, environmental engineers, and contingency and crisis management planners for a safe and secure work environment.

The treasurer is primarily concerned with financial risk management, driven largely by the volatility of interest rates, foreign exchange, and commodity prices. Specific risk management techniques, including the use of such derivative instruments as forwards, futures, swaps, and options, were discussed in Chapter 7.

Current techniques include value-at-risk and enterprise risk management.

- *Value-at-risk* (VaR) calculates the risk exposure in a portfolio of financial assets based on historical price patterns. Various proprietary models attempt to measure risk covariance to a selected degree of statistical confidence. VaR focuses on lines of business that involve high risk or investment, yet result in low returns. There are two significant problems in using VaR:

  1. Risks for which pricing is not available and may not be adequately considered; for example, the political risk of a coup d'état or currency devaluation in a foreign country, such as the 2002 situation in Argentina when the country defaulted on its international loans and faced credit and political crises.

  2. The "perfect storm" problem, when risks that normally are offsetting are concurrently adverse. A recent example is the collapse of Long-Term Capital Management (in 1998), when illiquid markets and political tensions caused the prices of U.S. Treasury securities to exceed historical trends.

- *Enterprise risk management* (ERM) attempts to integrate multi-source risks in a comprehensive organizational strategy. This

ERM at Hallmark Cards, Inc.

One consumer products company (Hallmark Cards, Inc.) that uses ERM has implemented a multistep process: identification of the risk, measurement, formulation of a cost-effective containment strategy, implementation of tactics to effectuate the strategy, and continuous monitoring. The company is supported by the services and technology of a major insurance broker, Marsh & McLennan.

approach considers risk as ubiquitous, requiring the coordination of all relevant business and political situations. For example, the Ford–Bridgestone–Firestone tire recall (in 2000) would normally escape traditional risk management oversight, but would be captured in a comprehensive ERM program that evaluates potential business risks. ERM analysis includes the risk of a significant product defect by assigning probabilities and worst-case scenario assumptions to specific situations that could significantly impact a company.

Control and Management of Disasters

The problem of control is present in all treasury functions and may be of greater concern today than in previous eras. This is due to several reasons:

- Staff downsizing, which compromises the separation of accounting and financial duties
- Technology advances, with an accompanying explosion in the exchange of data through interfaces supported by computers, telecommunications, and the Internet
- A general crisis in corporate governance, as employees, stockholders, and customers watch trusted institutions fail to protect the integrity of the financial system

- The failure of business to assign responsibility for protecting the most important "new" economy resource—not cash nor any physical asset—but intellectual capital

Employees

Employees represent a significant treasury threat, as they are inside the organization, know the security measures utilized in most areas (or lack of security), and may be difficult to detect in any wrongdoing. They may be hostile for various reasons, such as a perception of injustices against themselves or their colleagues, the desire for financial gain, "the challenge," or simply boredom. Bank products discussed throughout this book work well when properly administered, but may be circumvented by a determined individual and/or collusion.

Defenses against adverse employee actions include the following:

- Hire responsible, trustworthy employees, including clerical workers who may be selected or transferred to treasury with minimal background checking. It is the office staff with access to treasury information systems that can commit theft or fraud. Bonding of employees in positions with significant fiscal responsibility is a popular trend.

- Monitor employees who are in sensitive positions for changes in behavior or attitude due to financial problems, family strain, addictions or psychological illnesses, or other stresses. The format can be simple observation (e.g., conspicuous spending, personal telephone calls, workplace absences, changes in physical appearance) to more structured programs, such as mandatory personal financial statements and periodic medical exams.

- Although it may be distasteful, consider electronic surveillance of telephone calls and e-mail messages. Court findings are inconsistent as to whether employees can be subject to such scrutiny, as the law is still developing on privacy rights, although, increasingly, courts are ruling in favor of companies' right to monitor employee use of company-owned computers.

Electronic Devices and Barriers

A breach of security can occur at various points: accessing hardware or software, in telecommunications lines, and at banks or other vendors. Merely enclosing a facility and using guards or watchdogs does not adequately safeguard technology. Security must begin with entry restrictions to areas using electronic devices and barriers. Access to treasury information systems involves identification of the user with a password, a special badge or key, or a scan of the eye or fingerprint (biometrics).

The exchange of data between bank and company computers may involve multiple telecommunications connections. The resulting exposure from these possible points of intrusion has resulted in numerous occurrences of eavesdropping and theft. Communications should be required to pass a firewall barrier, to protect internal traffic from outsiders (or internal systems from each other), with all messages examined and entry barred if predetermined criteria are not met. In addition, telecommunications cables should be encased in steel or pressure-sensitive conduits that signal when there has been an intrusion on the line.

Computer and telecommunications systems can be protected by scanning programs to detect intrusions by:

- *Computer virus infections.* Viruses can be monitored by observing:
  - Processing time slowdowns
  - Programs trying to write to write-protected media
  - Unexplained computer memory decreases
  - Files that cannot be located
  - Unusual computer messages
  - Differences in length between active and archival files

- Use of unauthorized passwords or repeated password attempts
- Efforts to enter systems for which the user is not authorized
- Log-ons at an unusual time of day or on weekends
- Significant deviations in patterns of usage

Antivirus programs should be enabled to run automatically at regular intervals. The most recent versions of this type of software run constantly, in the background.

Disaster Recovery

Prior to the events of September 11, 2001, disaster recovery concerns focused on whether banks had a dedicated disaster recovery or contingency planning manager; a comprehensive plan listing precise steps in the event of a disaster; adequate technology support; automatic hardware, software, and telecommunications switching; and power backup, including dual power feeds and auxiliary power systems. Although those actions are still relevant, other considerations should be included in catastrophe planning, including actions by both the bank and the company.

- *Prevention.* Do the bank and the company have adequate physical security including detection and protection systems? Are there established procedures for control and access? Is regular data back-up required for all systems and data files, and are the media archived to a secure off-site location?

- *Evaluation and mobilization.* In a disaster recovery incident, who are the company and bank managers? Is there a specific plan for critical functions, such as hardware, software, technical support, and communications? What expectations are there for resumption of processing and restoration of the primary site? Is there a regular testing program of established procedures? Has the bank experienced an actual disaster? If so, what was the result? What steps has it taken to remedy any deficiencies in the plan?

- *Back-up site recovery.* Are the back-up sites sufficiently distant as to be unaffected by the disaster? Have arrangements been made with a third-party disaster recovery vendor, such as Comdisco or IBM?

Your bank will not share specific plans and procedures with its corporate customers; nevertheless, you should feel satisfied that the bank and your company is totally prepared for just about any attack or natural calamity that may occur.

Computer Security

Despite the planning for disaster, the attacks on September 11, 2001, disrupted typical corporate life for weeks, impacting nearly everyone who had to be in daily contact with their bankers. Most affected treasury managers were able to function using a back-up site or other facility.

IN THE REAL WORLD

Mutual Back-Up Sites

After September 11, 2001, many companies that were not directly affected by the disaster generously offered their crippled competitors floor space and equipment, pending their ability to reestablish independent facilities. Although these accommodations had not been agreed to by formal arrangement, they were successful due to the similarities of the business and/or the technological platforms. This has led to an increasing number of companies establishing mutual back-up sites with traditional but geographically remote competitors, providing an alternative solution to more costly, redundant back-up facilities.

ESSENTIALS of Managing Corporate Cash

TIPS & TECHNIQUES

Protecting Your Computer's Valuable Information

Here are some ideas to consider for protecting your computer and the valuable information it contains, such as bank account numbers, key company contacts, account balances, investments, pending debt or equity deals, or other financial matters.

- *Conceal laptops.* Any observant thief can spot a laptop; the shape of the briefcase is distinctive. Put the computer in a bag that doesn't look anything like computer luggage, such as a gym bag—no one wants to steal your dirty gym clothes.

- *Hide passwords and codes.* Don't put secret access information on a Post-it note on the computer, on the hard drive, or anywhere in the carrying case. Memorize it; or, if that's not convenient, keep it in a wallet but label it as, for example, a friend's phone number.

- *Encrypt files.* Several programs are commercially available to encrypt data, rendering files unreadable to anyone without a "key." The latest versions sell for about $50; they are well worth the expense when working with files that contain sensitive information.

- *Keep the computer in sight at all times.* Bags are often left unattended in airports and hotels while the owner is buying a newspaper or is on the phone; two seconds is all it takes for the bag to disappear. When going through airport security, put the laptop through last and do not let it move into the X-ray machine until you are allowed to pass through the detector. If you are stopped for an additional security check, make sure the computer is in your line of vision at all times.

- *Securely lock the computer.* If you are forced to go to an emergency site (other than home), tether the computer to immov-

TIPS & TECHNIQUES CONTINUED

able furniture with a steel cable lock that fits in a slot in the machine. Though new colleagues at the site may be absolutely trustworthy, an intruder can grab a laptop and disappear in the time it takes to go to the bathroom or get a sandwich.

- *Back up data—frequently.* Many financial managers do not regularly back up data to alternate media, such as the main server or an external floppy or CD-ROM drive. This should be done before the computer is shut down—*every time* that new data is entered. Store the back-up copy in a separate location, otherwise, the thief could take the data, the computer, and the second copy. In an emergency, or while on the road, send copies of changed or new documents in an e-mail to the office.

- *Load applications only.* If possible, keep data on a central remote server on the Web and load only the applications that allow the retrieval of the information onto the laptop.

- *Keep vital contact information with the computer.* If a disaster occurs, and working from the laptop is the contingency plan, this will be effective only if there is also a record of all the necessary phone numbers and codes with the computer, including the numbers of the banks and their emergency sites. Keep a detailed list of everything that may be needed in the computer bag.

- *Let the banks know the company's plans.* Banks have devised various security and access codes to protect the company's assets, and they need to be fully informed of your emergency arrangements, alternative phone numbers, and other disaster recovery plans. They may require proof of identity before executing any significant transactions, such as wire transfers, particularly if the communications are routed to an alternative bank site. File contingency plans with them and review them every six months. Also, don't wait for a disaster to occur to test the plans for the first time. Arrange with the bank to test the plan, to ensure it functions smoothly.

Often, a second site is a laptop computer, which can provide access to bank account data and other information from home or any location with telephone service. Many New York and Washington treasurers reported that they grabbed their laptops and relocated, often to their homes or to company offices in safer locations. That said, this convenience could potentially be a "land mine" for the unsuspecting, because of the large potential loss: the data that resides on a laptop could be worth millions of dollars to a smart thief.

Organization of the Treasury Function

Technology is the driving force and enabler behind many of the changes in treasury. It is the timely availability of information that allows balance management to be consolidated, liquidity to be optimized, and global risks to be measured and monitored. This section discusses the role of technology in enabling some of the major trends in the organization of the treasury function.

Centralization through Shared Service Centers (SSCs)

When business units perform the same function throughout a company, such as payroll, there is an opportunity to eliminate the duplication by using an SSC. Often described as "insourcing," an SSC acts as an independent business bureau within the company to present a single interface to the internal and outside worlds. Companies have been using SSCs for legal staff, real estate management, advertising, and travel services for many years. Applications in treasury, accounts payable, and accounts receivable are more recent. In larger companies, the SSC may evolve to be the in-house bank for the internal entities of the company, undertaking all the foreign exchange and currency management. SSCs provide the company with economies of scale, rationalization, and streamlining of processes and functions.

There are several critical elements to developing a successful SSC:

- Efficient communications and technology infrastructure to provide common platforms, often involving enterprise resource planning (ERP) systems
- Responsiveness to the needs of business units, often attained through service level agreements (SLAs) to assure an acceptable level of performance
- An organizational commitment to centralization

The launch of the EMU and the euro (see Chapter 7) has been a major driver for companies establishing SSCs for treasury functions, to help them compete more effectively in the new regionalized global economy.

Enterprise Resource Planning (ERP)

ERP systems claim to offer a common technology platform throughout the company, between and across the business units. A key technology issue for treasurers has always been integration with underlying business systems to obtain risk and exposure information for senior management reports. In theory, enterprisewide systems offer end-to-end business processing, from data input at the raw data level of accounts payable and receivable through inventory management, order processing, working capital management, and currency forecasting. Major providers of ERP systems are SAP, Oracle, J.D. Edwards, SunGard, and PeopleSoft.

In reality, implementation of an ERP system is time-consuming, difficult, and expensive. Companies often compromise the integrity of the concept by using one system for some functions and other systems for specialized areas such as treasury, or by having different versions of the software on different platforms. Both situations force further internal integration of systems. Another key technology issue is that ERP systems require an interface to external sources such as electronic banking and market information systems. While banks are increasingly try-ing to provide so-called plug-and-play interfaces with the major systems used by their clients, the evolving nature of the technology makes full compatibility difficult. ERP systems are likely to remain a viable tool for only the largest companies.

Outsourcing

Once a function has been centralized, the treasurer is in a position to determine whether there is an opportunity to outsource noncore func-tions. The decision has been made easier thanks to the proliferation of application service providers (ASPs) and business service providers (BSPs) offering Internet-based applications and services. ASPs allow a company to outsource particular operations, such as netting and treasury workstation routines. BPSs will undertake entire functions, such as the back-office processing of a cash management operation.

The justification for outsourcing is that a specialized third-party provider can perform the function more cost-effectively and with greater expertise and specialized technology investment than the company. Some of the benefits that can be expected are reduced exposure to technology shifts and market changes, reduced overhead and operating costs, and the freeing of internal resources and technology dollars for investment in core businesses. Outsourcing provides a turnkey solution and the expec-tation that the partner will retain a high level of expertise and leading edge solutions. The major concerns with outsourcing are the relinquish-ing of control and information to an outside party and a potential loss of flexibility caused by being tied to the partner's technology.

Open Architecture Electronic Banking (EB)

Companies are increasingly intolerant of proprietary formats and expensively integrated systems that tie them to a single bank's system. Several bank-neutral platforms, such as GEIS and BankLink, have been introduced to offer the flexibility of standardized interfaces with multiple bank EB platforms. This allows companies to change or add banks when necessary, without losing integrated interfaces. In Germany, the banks cooperated in developing a single EB platform called Multicash.

Future Role of the Treasurer

Over the last decade, the role of the treasurer has been elevated to the rank of strategic partner and key participant in the senior management team. When certain operational tasks are removed or outsourced, the treasurer becomes an advisor to the board on business strategy and global risk and liquidity management, hence effectively a "virtual treasurer" (Exhibit 10.2 illustrates the evolution of the treasury focus.)

Even though banking relationships are consolidated, and bankers are assured of profitability, treasurers will have to pursue credit alternatives to traditional lending: trade credit arrangements, seller financing, and

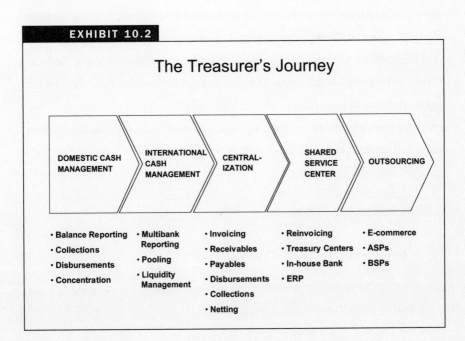

EXHIBIT 10.2

The Treasurer's Journey

DOMESTIC CASH MANAGEMENT	INTERNATIONAL CASH MANAGEMENT	CENTRAL-IZATION	SHARED SERVICE CENTER	OUTSOURCING
• Balance Reporting	• Multibank Reporting	• Invoicing	• Reinvoicing	• E-commerce
• Collections	• Pooling	• Receivables	• Treasury Centers	• ASPs
• Disbursements	• Liquidity Management	• Payables	• In-house Bank	• BSPs
• Concentration		• Disbursements	• ERP	
		• Collections		
		• Netting		

receivables factoring. Aggressive management of the working capital can minimize the cash conversion cycle (the number of days in the operating cycle less the payment period for expense factors).

Collection and disbursement activities should be rigorously scrutinized, as should the need to finance inventory through the implementation of just-in-time (JIT) procedures. Treasury must become the company consultant on cash and financial issues, to reduce dependence on credit facilities. In summary, treasurers will have to work harder and smarter, making certain that their banks receive adequate compensation and that their companies' operations are efficient and cost-effective.

Summary

The inevitability of financial change requires treasurers to be cognizant of new products, new regulations, and new opportunities to assist their organizations. Traditional U.S. cash management practice will become more electronic, and Internet-based technologies will drive the integration of accounting, treasury, sales, purchasing, and manufacturing systems. Bankers will use their scarce capital for profitable business opportunities, and will reduce their lending exposure while increasing pricing. This will force companies to call upon the skills of finance to be smarter in managing the working capital cycle. At the same time, risk management and security concerns have become critical considerations in managing company resources. The challenges and opportunities of the twenty-first century are indeed significant!

CASE STUDY

Bill and his staff are convinced that there are many economies of scale to be realized by centralizing certain functions in the cash management area. Some of the projects they are considering include:

- *A shared service center, building off the SSC that already exists for other functions in the company*

- *ASPs, which can provide an attractive alternative to developing in-house capabilities*

- *An intracompany netting system*

They do not think the company is ready for further outsourcing, as there is still considerable work to be done on centralizing, then determining the core competencies. Bill is not sure that he is comfortable with having a third party provide the interface for handling customer inquiries. In preparing for his meeting with the board of directors, Bill realizes that there is a lot of work to be done to prepare the treasury for the future.

Useful Sources

ASSOCIATIONS	WEB SITE
American Institute of Certified Public Accountants (AICPA)	www.aicpa.org
American Bankers Association (ABA)	www.//aba.com
Association for Corporate Treasurers (ACT)	www.corporate-treasurers.co.uk
Association for Financial Professionals (AFP)	www.afponline.org
Bank Administration Institute (BAI)	//bai.org
Euro Banking Association	www.abe.org
Financial Executives Institute (FEI)	www.fei.com
Local AFP/cash management associations	www.afponline.org
National Automated Clearing House Association (NACHA)	www.nacha.org

BANKS	WEB SITE
AmSouth	www.amsouth.com
Bank of America	www.bankamerica.com
Bank of New York	www.bankofny.com
Bank One	www.bankone.com
BB&T	www.bbandt.com
Citibank	www.citibank.com
Comerica	www.comerica.com
Fifth Third Bank	www.53.com
Fleet Boston	www.fleet.com
Harris Bank/Bank of Montreal (Canada)	www.harrisbank.com
J.P. Morgan Chase	www.jpmorganchase.com
Key Bank	www.keybank.com
M&T Bank	www.mandtbank.com
Mellon Bank	www.mellon.com
National City Bank	www.nationalcity.com

BANKS	WEB SITE
Northern Trust	www.ntrs.com
PNC Bank	www.pncbank.com
Regions Bank	www.regions.com
State Street Bank	www.statestreet.com
SunTrust Bank	www.suntrust.com
U.S. Bank	www.usbank.com
Union Bank of California	www.uboc.com
Wachovia Bank	www.wachovia.com
Wells Fargo	www.wellsfargo.com

FOREIGN GLOBAL BANKS	WEB SITE
ABN-AMRO (The Netherlands)	www.abnamro.com
Deutsche Bank (Germany)	www.deutsche-bank.com
HSBC (Great Britain)	www.hsbc.com

GENERAL INFORMATION	WEB SITE
Barrons	www.barrons.com
Business Finance	www.businessfinance.com
BusinessWeek	www.businessweek.com
Forbes	www.forbes.com
Fortune	www.fortune.com
Global Treasury News (United Kingdom)	www.gtnews.com
Gold Sheets	www.loanpricing.com
Institutional Investor	www.iimagazine.com
Phoenix Hecht	www.phoenixhecht.com
The Treasurer (United Kingdom)	www.treasurers.org
Treasury and Risk Management	www.treasuryandrisk.com
Bloomberg	www.bloomberg.com
International Treasurer (United Kingdom)	www.intltreasurer.com
Treasury Management International (United Kingdom)	www.treasury-management.com
Wall Street Journal	www.wsj.com

GOVERNMENT	WEB SITE
The Federal Reserve	www.federalreserve.gov
Federal Deposit Insurance Corp. (FDIC)	www.fdic.gov

GOVERNMENT	WEB SITE
Federal Reserve Bank of New York	www.ny.federalreservebank.org
Office of the Comptroller of the Currency (OCC)	www.occ.treas.gov
Securities and Exchange Commission (SEC)	www.sec.gov

SERVICE PROVIDERS	WEB SITE
Automatic Data Processing, Inc. (ADP)	www.adp.com
BankLink	www.banklink.com
Bolero.net	www.bolero.net
Currenex	www.currenex.com
ECCHO	www.eccho.com
Electronic Data Systems Corporation (EDS)	www.eds.com
Export-Import Bank	www.exim.gov
First Data	www.firstdatacorp.com
FXall	www.fxall.com
General Electric Information Services (GEIS)	www.geis.com
GTE Processing	www.gtedataservices.com
Identrus	www.identrus.com
Interpay	www.interpay.com
JD Edwards	www.jdedwards.com
Magnet Communications	www.magnetbanking.com
National Data Corp (NDC)	www.ndctech.net
National Processing Company (NPC)	www.npc.net
Oracle	www.oracle.com
Paychex	www.paychex.com
PeopleSoft	www.peoplesoft.com
Politzer and HANEY	www.ph.com
SAP	www.sap.com
SunGard	www.sungard.com
SWIFT	www.swift.com
Trade Card	www.tradecard.com
World Bank	www.worldbank.org

NACHA Formats

Cash Concentration or Disbursement Plus Addenda (CCD+)	Together with the Cash Concentration and Disbursement message (CCD), this format is used by cash managers to concentrate and disburse funds between companies. CCD+ has the additional benefit of allowing up to 80 characters of descriptive information. CCD allows space for a reference number only.
Corporate Trade Exchange (CTX)	This format was designed for payments that require substantial accompanying information. It uses a standard ACH payment transaction type to allow it to flow through the banking system, but incorporates the Accredited Standards Committee (ASC) X12 data standard in the electronic envelope. The ASC X12 message is a cross-industry electronic data interchange (EDI) format that can accommodate 9,999 records of up to 80 characters each of remittance information.
Prearranged Payment or Deposit (PPD)	This message type is consumer-oriented and is primarily used to authorize credit or debit transactions, often for recurring and fixed-amount payments, such as mortgage payments, insurance premiums, and direct deposit of payroll.

Re-Presented Check (RCK)	Items under $2,500 drawn on a consumer account that are rejected or returned may be represented through the ACH using the RCK message format.
Tax Payment Banking Convention Record Format (TXP)	This message type was designed for corporate state tax payments. It contains the data format for taxpayers to pay state taxes through the ACH. The format carries an 80-character addendum record field.

SWIFT Message Types

MT 100	A customer request to transfer funds (to be replaced by the MT103 in 2003).
MT 101	A customer payment request, debiting an account with a third-party bank. The initial receiving bank acts as a carrier of the instruction only.
MT 102	A payment instruction containing multiple transactions.
MT 103	Destined to replace the MT 100 by November 2003. The MT 103 is a more extended and structured version of the MT 100, designed to enhance automation and improve certainty and transparency of customer credit transfers.
MT 105, MT 106	EDIFACT envelopes to convey an EDIFACT message. The MT 106 is an extended version of the MT 105.
MT 110	Provides details of a check referred to in the message.
MT 200	A request from a financial institution to transfer funds from one of its accounts to another of its accounts with a different bank.
MT 202	Also known as a *cover payment*. This is an instruction from a bank to transfer funds to another bank.
MT 210	Also referred to as an *advice* or *notice to receive*. This message provides advance notice to the receiving bank that it will receive funds to be credited to a beneficiary account.
MT 300 series	Supports foreign exchange and money market transactions.
MT 500 series	Supports securities transactions.

MT 700 series	Supports trade and letter-of-credit transactions.
MT 940	Used for sending detailed customer transaction and balance reports.
MT 942	Used for intraday reporting of transaction detail.
MT 950	A financial institution statement message. Often used to send summary customer balance information.

Suggested Readings

Keith Checkley, *Cash Is Still King,* Fitzroy Dearborn Publishers, 2000.

———, *Strategic Cash Flow Management,* Capstone Publishing/John Wiley & Sons, Inc., 2002.

Dimitris N. Chorafas, *Liabilities, Liquidity, and Cash Management: Balancing Financial Risk,* John Wiley & Sons, Inc., 2001.

Frank J. Fabozzi (Ed.), *Cash Management: Products and Strategies,* John Wiley & Sons, Inc., 2000.

Daniel L. Gotthilf, *Treasurer's & Controller's Desk Book,* AMACOM Books, 2001.

Alastair Graham, *Cash Flow Forecasting and Liquidity,* Glenlake Publishing, 2000.

Jarrod V.T. Harford, *Corporate Cash Management, Excess Cash, and Acquisitions,* Garland Publishing, 1999.

Les Masonsen (Ed.), *Pratt's Corporate Treasury Management,* A.S. Pratt & Sons, 2000.

D.J. Masson (Ed.), *Essentials of Cash Management,* Seventh Edition, Association for Financial Professionals, 2001.

Bill McGuinness, *Cash Rules: Learn & Manage the 7 Cash-Flow Drivers for Your Company's Success,* Kiplinger Books, 2000.

James Sagner, *Cashflow Reeengineering,* AMACOM Books, 1997.

———, *Financial and Process Metrics for the New Economy,* AMACOM Books, 2001.

———, *The Real World of Finance,* John Wiley & Sons, Inc., 2002.

Brian Welch (Ed.), *Electronic Banking and Treasury Security,* CRC Press, 1999.

Index